powerselling

SEVEN STRATEGIES FOR CRACKING THE SALES CODE

GEORGE LUDWIG

Dearborn™
Trade Publishing
A **Kaplan Professional** Company

Vice President and Publisher: Cynthia A. Zigmund
Acquisitions Editor: Michael Cunningham
Senior Project Editor: Trey Thoelcke
Interior Design: Lucy Jenkins
Cover Design: Jody Billert
Typesetting: the dotted i

Published by Dearborn Trade Publishing
A Kaplan Professional Company

Library of Congress Cataloging-in-Publication Data

Ludwig, George.
    Power selling : seven strategies for cracking the sales code / George Ludwig.
       p.   cm.
    Includes bibliographical references and index.
    ISBN 0-7931-8571-8
    1. Selling.   2. Sales personnel.   3. Success in business.   I. Title.
HF5438.25.L83 2004
658.85—dc22

                        2004003271

ADVANCE PRAISE FOR *POWER SELLING*

In today's changing sales environment, salespeople must either grow or go. This book is a treasury of tips and techniques for helping salespeople bring greater value to their customers.

—RICK PAGE
Author of #1 sales bestseller,
Hope Is Not a Strategy: The 6 Keys to Winning the Complex Sale

I was reluctant to change Betco's selling process, but when we converted to the Power Selling system; our numbers began to climb faster than I had ever seen them in over seven years!

—DAN CARR
Vice President of Sales, Betco Corporation

In the fast-paced sales world, character can often be overlooked. George Ludwig walks you through the selling process from the inside out! When you think you know all the sales techniques there are to know, Power Selling gives you more to think about.

—MICHAEL SINGLETARY
NFL Hall of Famer, Linebacker Coach for the Baltimore Ravens, and partner in Singletary & DeMarco's Leadership Zone

This book shows you how to supercharge yourself and put your sales career onto the fast track.

—BRIAN TRACY
Author, Goals!

Power Selling *is not what I call "fluff." It's a "been in the trenches" formula for becoming successful in a very challenging field—sales. Nothing is sugar coated here. You'll get the real story from someone who has walked the talk.*

—DANIELLE KENNEDY
Speaker, sales trainer, and author of 7 Figure Selling

This book will give you the information, knowledge, and wisdom you need to master your sales career.

—NIDO QUBEIN
Chairman, Great Harvest Bread Company Founder, National Speakers Association Foundation

Power Selling *is a simple, yet powerful approach to becoming a sales superstar. Follow the Seven Critical Best Practices and your sales will soar.*

—TODD DUNCAN
Bestselling author of High Trust Selling

Many authors write books full of examples, but few actually lead by them. Power Selling *proves that success and sincerity really do go hand-in-hand. George is poised to take his place among the cream of the crop—Blanchard, Maxwell, Ziglar, Covey, and now Ludwig.*

—MARGARET MCALLISTER
President, McAllister Communications

A valuable, highly readable addition to the body of top-tier advice in professional selling. Bravo!

—STEPHAN SCHIFFMAN
Author, *Getting to Closed*

George has given our sales teams a simple but powerful new tool to build upon the tips given in Wise Moves. *We look forward to using* Power Selling *with all the members of our surgical specialty sales groups. Its clear, easy-to-understand messages will get results, even with professionals whose primary language is not English.*

—FRANCIS BOERO, PH.D.
Regional Director, Latin America
Johnson & Johnson Medical Devices & Diagnostics Group

This book is a must-read! George Ludwig has put together an insightful, practical sales book that even the most experienced salesperson can learn from.

—FRANK BUCARO, CSP, CPAE
Author of *Taking the High Road:*
How to Succeed Ethically When Others Bend the Rules

Don't put off reading this book! If you read only one book this year to improve your sales, this is it. Here's what you've been looking for—a simple and powerful strategy for sales success and financial abundance.

—RITA EMMETT
Author of *The Procrastinator's Handbook* and *The Procrastinating Child*

George Ludwig has compiled a history of sales techniques and converted it into a concise and entertaining road map for sales success. Power Selling *is a virtual encyclopedia, the "ABCs" of strategic selling and effective life skills. This is recommended reading not only for my team, but for any salesperson who wants to be a superstar.*

—JERRY VOGEL
Vice President Sales, Masimo Corporation

Realize your highest performance . . . use what's in this book.

—ANTHONY PARINELLO
Wall Street Journal bestselling author of *Selling to VITO*

Dedicated to Moomy Doll

C o n t e n t s

Thousands of books have been written on the art of selling. Just when you think you've read and heard it all, someone comes along and sets a new standard that revolutionizes the profession. That someone is George Ludwig, and his book, *Power Selling: Seven Strategies for Cracking the Sales Code,* teaches sales from a dynamic perspective that quickly puts you head and shoulders above the competition. He distills more than two decades' worth of sales success into seven powers that are easily understood and highly effective in their application. This book is both fun to read and worthwhile to use.

But *Power Selling* is not *just* a book of sales techniques. It goes beyond the selling profession to examine the person underneath the techniques, the character of salespeople themselves. It looks at your development as a person and shows how personal growth will lead not only to greater sales, but to greater significance and fulfillment. *Power Selling* helps you see the "big picture," and I can attest that nothing is more powerful in your life than having a compelling sense of purpose.

—Les Brown, Emmy-award-winning speaker,
bestselling author, and Mamie Brown's baby boy

Even though I didn't fully realize it at the time, the seed of desire to write this book was planted in my heart in 1979, when I entered the profession of selling and simultaneously made the commitment to make something out of my life. That seed of *desire,* whose Latin root literally means *of the father,* was planted by God. So eternal thanks go to God for giving me the desire to be all I can and to inspire and teach others to do the same.

Thanks also go to my own dad for being such a great role model for me. He taught me honesty, integrity, and a love of people and of making them laugh, qualities that form the core of a truly great salesperson. Thanks to my mother for loving me, believing in me, and listening to me from childhood all the way to my current calling. Thanks to Diana Kozerski and her daughters for their love and friendship. Thanks to my brother, Steve Ludwig, and his wife, Loui, for their unwavering love and for their own commitment to help others improve their lives.

A gigantic thank you goes to my loving sister, editor-in-chief, and writing partner, Sue Ann Burchill, who performed miracles under pressure by taking my ideas and unpolished words and transforming them into significantly better prose. Her husband, Tim, also provided invaluable insights.

Huge thanks go to Kyle Witt, Todd Hunt, Ken Semmler, and Mark Peterschmidt for their friendship and valuable feedback. A big hand must be extended to the very talented Becky Keen, who improved every page with her razor-sharp proofreading.

Thanks to thousands of salespeople whom I have worked alongside, observed, managed, trained, or read about in my quest to bring you the best-of-the-best sales strategies. Thanks to the great companies for whom I've had the privilege to sell or manage: the Kirby Company, Chevrolet, Patterson Dental Company, CooperVision, Physio-Control, Nellcor, Century 21, Haemonetics, and Johnson & Johnson. Special thanks to Indiana University for providing a solid business education and for continuing to hold high the bar of educational excellence.

In no particular order, I thank the following individuals who, in one way or another, contributed to the development of this book, whether they realize it or not: Mark Stasiulis and family, Jack Pluta, Steve Dority and family, John and Joe Gabriel, Scott Hoffman, Dan Carr, Greg Pastrick, Carlos Quiroga, John Abdo, Chad Seedorf, John Reed, Paul Betz, Greg Chesnutt, Joe Contrera, Kevin Mosher, David Engwall, Bill Davis, Tom Spencer, Denny Olsen, Jim Mazzarella, Ralph Germscheid, Art Berg, The HQ-Walden Staff, Donna Corr, Lillian Nicoletti, Jon Cole, Ruth Shumaker, Jay Stone, George Otto, Hank Brackman, Erik Nordstrom and Rick DeMarco.

Thanks go to the special mentors who have inspired me to help others break through to greater achievement, fulfillment, prosperity, and happiness—Zig Ziglar, Wayne Dyer, Anthony Robbins, Les Brown, Jim Rohn, Brian Tracy, Bill Hybels, and John Ortberg.

Thanks to the many audiences and companies who have hired me as a consultant, author, speaker, or trainer. I am very grateful to Rita Emmett and Mark Victor Hansen for their support and knowledge and for being awesome role models in my journey to become a best-selling author. Thanks to the many members of the National Speakers Association who have inspired me, educated me, and supported me. Huge thanks and great respect go to Jane Jordan Browne, who saw potential in me and this book. Very big thanks go to Danielle Egan-Miller, my literary agent, and her staff for nurturing this project and finding a great publisher.

A warm and heartfelt thank you goes to my publisher, Dearborn Trade Publishing, and their excellent staff for bringing this book to life. Roy Lipner, Cynthia Zigmund, Michael Cunningham, Trey Thoelcke, and the entire Dearborn staff deserve a round of applause for being professional and easy to work with.

The creation of this book has been an odyssey, sprinkled with many well-timed miracles, in which I have grown in the process. Words just don't do justice to the gratitude I feel—thank you, and God bless you all!

CRACKING THE CODE

In the end, it is important to remember that we cannot become what we need to be by remaining what we are.

—MAX DE PREE

Five years into my sales career, I had read dozens of books on sales and selling. I memorized the techniques and scripts touted by Tom Hopkins, Zig Ziglar, Brian Tracy, and most of the rest of the nation's leading sales trainers during that era. I listened to motivational audiotapes and attended national seminars, but I couldn't get the results I craved. I *hate* when that happens.

Then I met Bill.

Bill accelerated his metallic gray Porsche away from the curb, and we sped out of the hospital's parking lot. Bill had just sold several hundred thousand dollars' worth of cardiac monitoring equipment to a Chicago hospital. The year was 1984, and Bill was the first sales superstar I'd ever met. Bill sold circles around both his fellow salespeople and the competition.

Bill was my boss for a position I had just accepted, where I would sell medical equipment in the hospital marketplace. We made many sales calls together, and by all the standard ways of measuring persuasiveness—my use of logic, my presentation skills, my overall approach—I should have been every bit as persuasive as Bill. But was I? Not even close! And I *hate* when that happens.

Bill was phenomenal. He just happened to sell hospital equipment, but he could have sold absolutely anything. He was a consistent national sales champion and made a pile of money. He was the master of friendly persuasion. With just a smile and a handshake, he was powerful, contagious, and irresistible to buyers old and new. People just wanted to agree with him. Certainly Bill was likeable. His energy, enthusiasm, and charm were apparent. But his success on the job, his success *selling*, came from something else. I wanted what he had. I wanted to be able to sell like he did, smiling all the way to the bank, but I didn't have a clue what made him such a superstar. And *boy*, do I hate when that happens.

Bill sent me on a quest that day in 1984. He became my "white whale," if you will—my obsession to figure out what makes a sales superstar tick. For the next 15 years, I studied every great salesperson I encountered. I observed their habits, pestered them with endless questions about *how* they did what they did, and analyzed the effects of their sales techniques. I read more than 200 books by top sales gurus. I field-tested every sales tip that came my way. I sold like crazy. I sold greeting cards, vacuum cleaners, automobiles, real estate, dental chairs, contact lenses, cardiac defibrillators, and $100,000 low-temperature hydrogen peroxide sterilization systems. I sold $1 items, and I sold a contract representing over $14 million in sales. I sold in New York, California, and almost every state in between. Sometimes I received huge commission checks, and sometimes I wondered where my next meal would come from, but I just kept selling. I kept selling and studying and researching—until I finally figured it out. Now, I *love* when that happens.

After two decades in the sales profession, I finally understood what made Bill the champion he was. It wasn't what he said to people or any specific technique he used. It was *how* he talked and acted. He, and all the other sales stars, possessed a unique set of powers, or strategies, that they used reflexively, often unconsciously. These strategies resulted from the fusion of their extensive knowledge, their great skills, and their superior outlook—and that combination was always greater than the sum of the parts. These powers were so consistent across top salespeople, it became obvious to me that they were simply part of sales superstars' makeup, part of their sales DNA.

It might seem that my quest was over and my obsession would end. After all, I had achieved my goal, I'd reeled in the big one, and I'd become a master seller myself. But my moment of insight, my "aha" experience, was so compelling that I undertook a driving new passion—to share the fruits of my labors with you. The seven powers that I discovered are not esoteric pearls of wisdom, only comprehensible by an elite few. They're simple strategies that produce extraordinary results for ordinary salespeople. My mission is to give you the benefits of my 25 years of selling, managing, and training so that you can turn yourself into one of the greats—without having to put in all my years of work. I love when *that* happens, too.

Power Selling is my vehicle to deliver the goods. It will give you the top seven sales strategies that the superstars use—the best of the best. They represent the 20 percent of all sales activities that produce 80 percent of the results. They're easy to learn and remember, which means you're more likely to apply them to your own career and make your own pile of money. *You're* gonna love when that happens.

Power Selling also offers you a unique chance to figure out which of the seven powers are your strengths and which ones you need to work on. Log on to http://www.powersellingbook.com to complete our online Power Selling Assessment Questionnaire. These 105 questions can be answered in just a few minutes and will provide you with a progress report that you can use to map out your own journey to become a sales superstar. Fill out this assessment *before* you read the rest of the book, so you'll know better which chapters to really zero in on.

Power Selling will also provide you with a proven sales process that allows you to organize these principles and apply them to your own selling situations. This system sequences all that you learn in this book into a logical framework that is easily repeatable. It shows you *what* you need to do and *when* you need to do it in any given sales scenario.

In 1953, two young researchers in England, James Watson and Francis Crick, deciphered the structure of DNA. Their work has been heralded as a major breakthrough. Science has now successfully identified and ordered most of the more than three billion molecular letters residing inside every human cell. Cracking the human genetic code—the chemical blueprint of our physiology—opened a door of great promise for curing diseases in the future.

Power Selling has cracked the sales code. It presents you with the DNA—the irreducible powers of success—that resides in every sales superstar. These powers—*reputation, real passion, research, rapport, resource management, resiliency,* and *relationships*—will move you from financial mediocrity to financial abundance. When you commit to the "gene therapy" of *Power Selling,* you're on the road to success. I know, because I've traveled it. These principles took me from flipping hamburgers at McDonald's in 1979, where I made less than $4 an hour, to the French Riviera in 1995. There, I sipped a martini (shaken, not stirred, of course) in a fine tuxedo as I celebrated a six-figure income for helping a start-up division of Johnson & Johnson reach $25 million in sales in its first year.

My mission is not finished until you break through to sales stardom and stroll down the red carpet to collect your own "Sales Oscar." And, man oh man, do I *love* when that happens.

THE POWER OF
REPUTATION

Invest in Your Identity

Who you are speaks so loudly, I cannot hear a word you're saying.
—ANONYMOUS

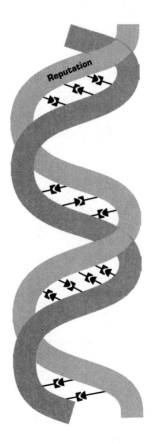

Name a well-known computer software company. If you're like more than 95 percent of Americans, you picked Microsoft. Name a long-distance telephone company. Most people choose AT&T. Name a well-known soft drink. I'll bet you selected what more than 90 percent of Americans picked—Coca-Cola. These companies enjoy the Power of Reputation. They've created and leveraged a credible identity in their markets, which creates trust and translates directly into increased sales success for these companies. The world's greatest salespeople, likewise, maximize the Power of Reputation by investing in their personal identities. They create a credible identity, live it consistently, then leverage it for the utmost results. The Power of Reputation occupies the top strand on the double helix of sales superstars' DNA, because it can influence others before we ever meet them.

On a Monday afternoon in 1998, the phone rang at Bill Topper's law office, and Sarah grabbed the call. Sarah, Bill's senior staff person, was very reluctant to bother him with what she thought might be a sales call. However, when she poked her head into the conference room to tell Bill that a "John G." was on the phone, Bill immediately excused himself and took the call in another room. Bill had never met John G., nor had he ever spoken with him, so why was he willing to interrupt his work to listen to this stranger suggest he place an ad on the back of the local phone book?

The simple reason was that, although Bill didn't know John G., he did know *of* him. John was a sales superstar in the telecommunications industry who sold advertising for Sprint Yellow Pages. He had worked with attorneys for more than a decade to design and place ads that often led to a substantial increase in business for their practices. Several of Bill's colleagues had used his services and spoken highly of him, so Bill took his call.

John suggested that they meet so he could showcase the value and design of the proposed ad, which would be quite expensive. Bill responded that because he knew of John's excellent reputation—including that his word was "as good as gold"—he trusted him enough just to put the order through over the phone. Keep in mind that this expression of faith was coming from a lawyer—a lawyer who had never even met John.

John objected, saying, "We'd better meet. The ad will probably run more than $55,000!"

The attorney then said something John would never forget. He said, "I don't care what the cost is. You know the business, and I know your reputation, so if you say do it . . . let's do it."

John wrote up that order, which helped him win his 12th consecutive National Sales Award and a Glamour Trip to Puerto Rico. John's use of the Power of Reputation gave him a sales edge that left his competitors holding an empty bag.

Sales superstars from every industry have stories just like John's that demonstrate the value of a reputation that blasts past the number-one barrier in all selling situations: more than 75 percent of people who need a product or service do not buy it because they're afraid of making a mistake. They're suspicious. Everyone has bought something and then later regretted it. Every buyer has at one time or another paid too much, gotten the wrong product, received lousy service, or been outright lied to by a salesperson. Buyers today have been exposed to virtually every possible con scheme, price manipulation, deception, quick ploy, maneuver, slight-of-hand, trick, and trap that's ever been used in the marketplace by a salesperson. "Joe Slick" and his clones are everywhere in the world of selling.

Because buyers carry heavy baggage from being burned by salespeople, they naturally remain skeptical and distrustful of every sales offer. That's why salespeople are forced to live by the Napoleonic Law: you're guilty until proven innocent. Salespeople are guilty, by association, of all the sins that other salespeople have committed. So, it bears repeating: *buyers are suspicious.* And well they should be. Very few salespeople, managers, and executives consider and plan for this fact.

So what's the best strategy to overcome buyer suspicion and skepticism? Sales masters know that it's the Power of Reputation. Having a reputation that's credible and trustworthy is the strongest antidote to this natural and normal problem. The Power of Reputation builds up the buyer's concept of the salesperson and his or her company as being believable and as selling a trustworthy product.

The Power of Reputation not only breaks through this major barrier to selling success, but, when leveraged fully, predisposes people to buy from you and your company before you ever meet them. You do want to condition potential buyers to buy from you before you ever meet them, don't you? Say yes, because it will significantly increase your earnings. To splice the Power of Reputation into your sales DNA, you have to build a credible personal identity, live it consistently to expand it into a reputation, and then leverage it to explode your sales results. In other words, you've got to *get* it, *live* it, and *leverage* it.

GET IT! BUILDING A SOLID PERSONAL IDENTITY

Employing the Power of Reputation to increase your sales begins with developing a strong, credible personal identity. You can't leverage your reputation for greater sales if you're seen by others as untrustworthy. Building a solid personal identity requires knowing who you are, believing you can always become better, and then making sure that you're credible.

Know Who You Are

Believe it or not, no matter how typical your life may seem to be up until now, your identity is complex. It's made up of the sum total of all your experiences; your understanding of those experiences; your beliefs about how the world operates; your attitudes about the past, present, and future; your skills and talents; and your ideas about how others see you. In any selling situation, you come armed with a complex interaction of those factors that influence how you behave with that client. To the extent that you can increase your own knowledge and understanding of yourself, you can increase your comfort with who you are—and this translates into an ease of manner to which your customers will immediately respond and trust. Although offering a comprehensive personal analysis is beyond the scope of this book, it's well worth the time to lay some groundwork for understanding who you are.

Start by taking stock of where you are in your selling career. Are you a ten-year veteran with a lot of success stories under your belt, or are you new to the profession? What motivates you the most right now? The desire to be *number one*? More income? Greater stability for your family? Maybe you're considering taking a sales position and just want to get a jump-start on what it takes to be successful. Or maybe you're just tired of mediocre results and finally motivated to have the breakthrough year you deserve.

What are your greatest strengths as a salesperson? Your biggest flaws? Is it discipline, perseverance, lack of preplanning, fear of rejection? How can you play to your strengths at the same time you improve your weaknesses? What kind of personality do you have? Outgoing? Introverted? Don't assume that all successful salespeople are inherently gregarious—some of the best say very little but make every word count.

What's your past been like? Have you done things you regret? Sometimes the past seems like a heavy ankle iron, but this book is about stepping away from that past to create a more favorable selling future. What goals do you have for that future? Where do you want to be in one year? In five? What support or assets do you have in achieving those goals? What barriers do you face?

Remember, at this point, your goal is to develop greater awareness of the kind of person you are and discover how that identity plays out in the selling arena. The online assessment referred to in the introduction will greatly help you understand your strengths and weaknesses as a salesperson. Get comfortable with who you are, and your identity will grow into a reputation that your buyers will love.

Believe You Can Be Better

In the process of uncovering who you are, you may determine that you want to change part of your identity. Then I have some good news—you can! No matter what's happened in your past, or where you are in your sales career evolution, it's never too early or too late to change. Sales superstars always believe they can build a better identity. This is not theory for me—this is my testimony.

When I was growing up, my ideas about who I was were based primarily on my size. I was the smallest kid in my school, weighing only 112 pounds at high school graduation. It always seemed to me that bigger was better, and because I was so little (I even got stuffed into a locker one time), what could I possibly accomplish? I never achieved much academically or athletically, because I didn't believe I had enough to offer.

Many years later, by doing some difficult self-development work, I finally began to see that my beliefs about myself did not have to be permanent. Ultimately, by believing I could change, I did. And that shift in my identity started a chain of events that led me eventually to achieve sales stardom, run a marathon, become a licensed pilot, help launch a new sales division for Johnson & Johnson, and build my own successful sales and peak performance consulting company (I never did get to date Miss Indiana, however). Building a solid identity requires an ongoing belief that you can always become better.

Remember this phrase: *your past does not equal your future.* What matters is not only knowing who you are now but also believing that, no matter where you've been or what shortcomings you have, you can always become better.

Make Sure You're Credible

The third component to a solid personal identity is to make sure that who you are is credible. In other words, you and the company you represent must be believable. Potential clients must be able to trust that you'll deliver what you say you'll deliver—a product or service that they can depend on.

Remember when Bill Clinton's 2001 grand jury testimony, about not having an affair with Monica Lewinsky, was found to be contrary to the evidence? The American people were outraged, and the implication was that he could not be trusted. Whether or not the implication was fair, it does make a valid point about buyer perception. If you can't convince potential buyers that you can be trusted, you're no better off than a president going through a grand jury indictment or any different from used-car salesperson "Slippery Sam" whose income is based on deceit. In a sales career, if long-term success is important to you, then establishing your trustworthiness is mandatory.

So what steps must you take to develop a credible personal identity? You must make an investment in yourself. Developing a more credible identity mandates self-improvement. Business philosopher Jim Rohn always says, "Better selling starts with a better you." Personal development precedes professional achievement in the world of sales—you've got to make deposits in the bank account called *you.*

Navy SEALS are the "best of the best." They're the tip of the spear for America's military—the fighting elite. SEALS are able to strike anytime, anywhere, without warning. They can come from under the sea, out of the air, and across the land. Why are they the best? Because the Navy, and the SEALS themselves, make a tremendous investment in their ongoing training and self-development. Today, it takes more than 30 months to complete just the initial training of a Navy SEAL, and for every trainee who succeeds, four fail. Those who make it excel in competence, confidence, commitment, and character every waking moment.

The selling elite, like the fighting elite, succeed only to the degree that they adhere to those same principles. Not everyone will invest enough in self-development to become a sales superstar, but those who do will become what the Marines call "the few, the proud," and what Navy SEAL Dick Couch calls "the courageous, the driven." They will have mastered the four building blocks of a credible identity—the C-CORE of *competence, confidence, commitment,* and *character.*

Competence comes by working every day to improve your performance and your knowledge of your business. It means you're an absolute expert in your chosen field, and there's no way to build credibility without it. You demonstrate your expertise as soon as you open your mouth for the first time with the buyer. Buyers can spot competent salespeople almost immediately by observing their manner, their appearance, their approach, and the quality and intelligence of their questions. How well you prepare for every detail of the meeting and the thoroughness with which you communicate are also crucial.

Success is a matter of luck. Ask any failure.
—EARL NIGHTINGALE

Having expertise in your field, however, is not enough. The buyer also must *perceive* you as competent. For better or worse, in business, appearance and image play a huge role. People are visual—buyers look for clues to determine how trustworthy and competent you are by the way you dress. More than 90 percent of the first impression you make on someone will be based on your clothes. For this reason, top producers dress for success. Bill, my first sales mentor, always said to spend twice the money and get half the number of garments. He said it was a wise move to spend more than you think you can afford for a suit but end up with a very high quality suit. In addition, if you happen to be a sales professional calling on high-level executives, you definitely need to exhibit a competent, executive image. You need to act like an executive by modeling yourself after the executives you are around. Study how they talk, listen, and make decisions, and then develop that kind of demeanor. You must look the part, too. Emulate their style and copy the quality of clothes they choose, what they drive—even down to what they take notes with. I say, "Dress for who you want to become, not who you are."

Confidence builds upon the competence that you've worked hard to develop. When you know that you're an expert and have thought through every detail of a sales encounter, and when you know that you're great at selling and capable of dealing with anything that may come up, it's easy to believe that buyers will trust you with their money—and they will. After you've read and assimilated the seven strategies of *Power Selling* and have cracked the sales code, your confidence will soar. You're probably thinking that my confidence must be pretty darn high to make such a bold statement—and it is. More than anything else, confidence emanates from your absolute conviction that your product or service is outstanding and well suited as a solution for your buyers. Your belief in yourself lends credibility to your identity as a trustworthy salesperson. Your strong conviction about the quality and value of what you're selling unleashes such an irresistible force, that buyers will be more likely to say yes, yes—and yes!

Commitment may not necessarily come easily for sales superstars, but they never leave it out of their identity. They don't involve themselves; they *commit* themselves—to the selling profession, their products, their ongoing personal development, serving their customers at the highest level, and, most of all, to maintaining excellence. Top sales producers will tell you that they became successful only after making a commitment to becoming one of the very best in their field. Once they committed, they put their focus on becoming great and didn't let up till they arrived. Sometimes it took months, or even years, for them to move ahead of the other salespeople in their field, but move ahead they did. Once they got ahead, they kept working harder, widening their lead. Eventually, they were winning Glamour Trips, cashing huge commission checks, and being honored by their companies and peers. It all started with commitment.

Lillian N., a nurse clinician for Johnson & Johnson, was given a rare opportunity to leave nursing and try her hand in sales in 1995. Most senior managers counted her out because her identity as a nurse (usually described as touchy-feely) with no sales experience didn't seem credible in the tough selling arena of Philadelphia.

What management had forgotten was that commitment also makes a major impact on identity, and Lillian had committed to becoming the best. That's exactly what she did. In less than two years, she went from being a nurse to strolling across the stage at the National Sales Meeting to collect her "Sales Oscar" for sales specialist of the year, with a tripled income. Her commitment to excellence resonated in everything she did and convinced buyers that they could trust her. She soon had a stellar reputation based on her commitment to excellence.

> *A man can never rise beyond the limitations of his own character.*
> **—JOHN MORLEY**

Character is the most important asset for a sales superstar's identity. When I was learning to play golf as a kid—long before the fancy, large-head clubs of today—my dad always instructed me to swing the club so that it hit the ball with the sweet spot of its face, making the ball go straighter, higher, and farther. Character is the sweet spot of your personal identity. It's what will make your sales numbers higher, your relationships with buyers longer, and trust in you go further. Nothing gives you greater credibility with buyers than your character—for while they'll tolerate occasional, honest mistakes, character "slip-ups" will violate their trust and make further sales virtually impossible.

Character traits such as honesty, integrity, a sense of fair play, and respect for others are absolutely vital for long-term success as a salesperson. Headline news in recent years about unethical business conduct by corporations such as Arthur Andersen, Enron, and WorldCom all make this point. Would you want someone with a cloud over his head, like Ken Lay, as your sales rep now? Top salespeople genuinely care about their customers and would never sell a product they didn't feel was right for the buyer. They know that their character is the number-one quality that buyers seek when making significant purchasing decisions, and this attitude keeps their clients in mutually satisfying, long-term relationships.

Top producers know that salespeople who take the money and run eventually find themselves holding an empty bag.

Your reputation is all about your personal identity—in sales, the initial product you're putting in front of people is yourself. To inspire the trust of your buyers, you'd better be putting out a product that stands above and beyond anything your competitors offer. Tremendous success awaits if you invest the time and effort to develop a strong personal identity.

Here's a list of Power Boosters for getting a strong personal identity and establishing credibility.

POWER BOOSTERS

- Spend at least two hours taking stock of your strengths and weaknesses as a salesperson, first to get comfortable with who you are, then to focus on improvement. (Complete the online assessment if you haven't already.)

- Commit today to the belief that it's a *must,* and not just a *should,* for you to become a true sales superstar. (Write it down.)

- Invest at least one hour a week in becoming more competent in your business/product/industry knowledge to increase your credibility.

- Become totally confident in your selling ability, and commit to excellence by mastering this book.

- Align and monitor your character traits so that you're honest and principle centered, and employ a win-win philosophy in all sales encounters.

- Go buy a new suit, dress, or other accessory to upgrade your image today.

LIVE IT! TURNING YOUR IDENTITY INTO A REPUTATION

Once you've got a strong, solid identity, it's time to turn that identity into a reputation. Impeccable character and great credibility won't affect your sales much unless the buyer knows that you have those assets. You've got to live out your identity consistently, in every facet of your life, and make sure prospective clients bump into that identity everywhere they turn. By building a *focus on serving* and becoming an *industry Headliner* (a term I'll discuss later in this chapter), your personal identity will bloom into a full-fledged reputation that will accelerate your sales.

Focus on Serving Buyers

"You can keep either car," Anies H., an auto salesperson from Isringhausen Imports, said to me on the phone. "If you want to keep your Carrera 2, that's fine, or if you want the 911 Turbo, you can have that. I'll drive away whichever car you don't want with no strings attached. No pressure either way!" I was contemplating purchasing a new car, and Anies was willing to drive more than 250 miles to bring me the new car, so that I could decide if I wanted to keep my black Porsche Carrera 2 or opt for a new red Porsche 911 Turbo. I was very much on the fence but definitely leaning toward keeping my current car. "Okay, bring it up," I said, figuring I had nothing to lose.

When that wide-bodied, red Porsche came rolling around the corner onto my street, I knew the decision wouldn't be as easy as I'd anticipated. Anies jumped out of the car with a big smile on his face, warmly extended his hand to shake mine, and then said, "George, you keep 'em both for 24 hours, and I'll pick up whichever one you don't want. By the way, you're already approved for the new one, too."

The Power of Reputation starts with your identity, but it won't take you very far if you don't focus on serving clients and buyers. Anies had a passion for serving his clients, and he knew that *great service* is the single biggest reputation builder salespeople can use to win more business. Most auto salespeople would never consider driving that distance for a prospect who was definitely undecided, especially one who was leaning the other way. But Anies knew that good buyers deserve to be "wowed" both during and after the sale. I was blown away—he made me feel like a king by bringing that car 250 miles right to my doorstep. Anies knew that real selling is always about serving. By the way, in case you were wondering . . . I bought that red Porsche 911 Turbo, and Anies walked away with a nice commission check. That car was sweet! (As you'll discover, I'm obsessed with Porsche.)

> *You make a living by what you get. You make a life by what you give.*
> **—SIR WINSTON CHURCHILL**

Sales superstars know that the word *sell* originates from the Scandinavian root *selzig*, which literally means *to serve*. Losing sight of this core principle by focusing on your commission, a quarterly sales quota, or closing a hot deal prevents many salespeople from becoming elite sellers. Sales pros serve their buyers so fervently that an almost unbreakable customer loyalty develops. They're completely devoted to satisfying the needs of those they serve. This focus on service becomes a powerful sales tool indeed, because satisfied buyers not only remain loyal but also tell others how they were treated. Nothing builds a reputation better than testimonials from satisfied customers.

How would your clients or buyers describe *your* level of service? If you focus and perform like salespeople from the following two companies, you can count yourself among the very elite. Nordstrom department store's salespeople are told, for example, "Use your own good judgment in all situations to make the customer happy." Their salespeople are legendary for going way beyond the call of duty. They've even gone to a competitor's store to buy a product for a customer if their store was out of the item. Just like Macy's in the movie *Miracle on 34th Street,* Nordstrom's amazes customers with its service and keeps them coming back for more.

Salespeople and customer service personnel from the Ritz-Carlton Hotel are taught, "If a customer complains to you, you own the problem, and you must resolve the problem—no matter whom you must involve to get the job done." Frank Bucaro, author of *Taking the High Road,* shares a funny story of when he arrived at a Ritz-Carlton and complained to the bellman of a very full bladder. Because of their policy for handling customer problems themselves, the bellman took Frank directly to the men's room himself. At the men's restroom door, Frank nervously asked, "You aren't coming in, are you?" The bellman replied, "No! No! Our service definitely stops at the door." Frank's story, though humorous, illustrates how an extraordinary level of service is not forgotten by a buyer or customer.

> *Be great in the little things.*
> **—GEORGE HERBERT PALMER**

Buyers who have experienced super service by a salesperson, or anybody else in a company, will tell others about their experiences. Word of mouth will accelerate the Power of Reputation, transforming it into the ultimate marketing tool for the salesperson. Recent data confirm that it is *seven* times as expensive to get a new buyer as it is to keep an existing one. Why spend all that effort getting new buyers to replace those you've lost to neglect? Focus on servicing your existing clients—it's a far easier way to build your sales career. Serving your buyers *after* the sale is what keeps them coming back, and mediocre salespeople routinely drop the ball in this area. Hey, you can't drop the ball and still make that glorious three-point basket from the top of the key. (As a Hoosier, I love basketball, even if I can't really play the game.)

Serving your clients at the highest level also means that they become members of *your* special club. Remember the jackets with the *Members Only* logo? When people buy from you, you want them to feel that they've purchased more than a product or service. Tops sales guns create this exclusive club by providing their customers with recognition and special treatment, which affirm each buyer's uniqueness and value. If you consistently recognize your buyers and make them feel special, like Anies did for me, they'll reward you with continuous business throughout your career.

Find ways to acknowledge the members of your club. Sometimes a personal gesture can pay off more handsomely than thousands of dollars in organized promotions. The world's greatest salespeople always apply the appropriate personal touch.

The selling elite don't just sell, they *initiate* buyers to their products or services after the sale. Initiating a product or service is teaching your buyers how to use what you sold them. It is installing your product or service so that buyers receive all the benefits they expected when they bought it. No matter what your line of business, devise a way to make your clients feel comfortable with what you sold them. Initiate buyers after the sale so they know you have a genuine interest in their well-being. This builds trust and leads to repeat business. Poor salespeople often abandon their buyers right after the sale and then cannot figure out why their repeat business is almost nonexistent. The Power of Reputation works both ways—it creates a negative ripple effect when we neglect our clients after the sale.

When you keep the primary focus on serving your buyers, you're investing in your identity. As you fully develop and communicate your commitment to provide outstanding service, the Power of Reputation kicks in, bringing you increased sales. Going beyond the call of duty, welcoming clients into your own special club, and initiating after the sale leverages your identity and builds a powerful reputation.

Be an Industry Headliner

His name is Joe Girard. He grew up in the Motor City, also known as Motown—Detroit, Michigan. He has the distinction of being the world's number-one car salesperson. His record of selling 1,425 new cars in one year still stands in the *Guinness Book of World Records*. They weren't fleet sales, either; they were individual units sold at retail, one at a time. How did Joe do it?

Joe knew that a major key to unleashing the Power of Reputation was to become a Headliner in his industry. Just like Frank Sinatra in Las Vegas, Joe became the *main event*—a Headliner—in Detroit's auto market. He forged an identity above the rest of the pack and promoted it relentlessly, until his reputation literally became a brand unto itself. He always wore a gold lapel pin that said *No. 1* on it, and he sent postcards out every month to his 13,000 former buyers with the same message—"I Like You!" Just as Muhammad Ali's constant mantra of "I'm the greatest!" showed up everywhere—on TV, on radio, in the ring, in person—and made him unforgettable, Joe's simple tactics gave him an unforgettable reputation with his customers. Sales superstars like Joe become headliners in their industry by being a *specialist* in their niche and by being *unique*.

Specialize in a market niche. Most sales executives from *Fortune* 100 companies agree that dominating a market niche—a well-defined market segment—wins more business. Concentrating your selling efforts in a single industry niche allows you to maximize your expertise, credibility, and reputation. Contacts know each other within an industry, and their networks allow your reputation to spread. You become much more visible, like Joe Girard did, thereby bolstering your reputation and getting you closer to becoming a Headliner. Knowledge of a single market also helps you sell more because you are *the* specialist. You have a reputation for being an expert authority in your niche and can provide references that your prospect will recognize. Buyers today have big challenges, and they want proven solutions from experts who understand the specific nuances of their problems. They don't want generalists. Imagine having an eight-year-old girl fall and break her arm in three places while riding her bike, like a close friend's daughter did. Was she taken to the family doctor, a general practitioner? No way! She went right to the best orthopedic surgeon in town.

It takes an orthopedic surgeon to set broken bones correctly, and it takes a sales specialist to provide the specific expertise that buyers need. When I was looking to buy investment property in Chicago's Lincoln Park in the 1980s, a local friend said that I had to talk with Chuck T. Chuck T. was "Mr. Lincoln Park" when it came to two-flat and three-flat rental properties. I called Chuck and arranged to meet him at his office. He stepped out of a gorgeous black Mercedes 450SL Coupe, impeccably dressed in an Italian suit, and opened the door for me to his richly appointed cherry wood office suite. Chuck had it going on! His office was lined with pictures of celebrity clients he'd served. I queried him on a couple of properties I had already looked at in the area to test his expertise.

Success comes when you do what you love to do,
and commit to being the best in your field.
—BRIAN TRACY

It quickly became apparent that Chuck knew more about those two properties, which I had been studying in detail, than I did, despite the fact that I had my real estate license. In fact, he knew *every* property within the confines of Lincoln Park. He knew their history and the nuances of their values street by street. The guy was simply amazing. He took being a specialist to the nth degree. He had the best-known reputation in Lincoln Park, which translated to selling more rental properties in Lincoln Park than anybody else. He focused on that tiny geography, scrupulously studied every single property, worked his tail off, and in the process became super well-known. The result: Chuck T. was the main event in Lincoln Park real estate—a Headliner—and he dominated that niche.

The strategy obviously paid off; last I heard, Chuck had retired at the ripe old age of 48.

Be unique. Joe Girard stood out. Muhammad Ali stood out. Top sales professionals know that if they can be unique, they'll be remembered by their buyers. This ability to stand out moves their identity into a reputation and enhances their sales success. A unique identity can be accomplished in many ways. Everything from personal monikers, trademark clothing, follow-up techniques, and personal marketing methods can help you be unique to your buyers.

> *We are all born unique, but most of us die copies.*
> **—ANONYMOUS**

Harvey B.—a telemarketing entrepreneur and sales professional from Wheeling, Illinois—is known as the "cookie man." Whenever Harvey finishes a sales call or follow-up visit, he gives his buyers or prospects one of his homemade chocolate chip cookies. People love his cookies (they're incredibly good), and they tend to remember Harvey because he brought them. When I was selling to hospitals in the early 1990s, purchasing agents said they loved to listen to my answering machine messages or the voice mails I left them, because they were always high energy, fun, and sometimes a bit crazy! What do you expect from a Hoosier? Larry King is known for the suspenders he wears. Donna C., a top sales producer at Johnson & Johnson's ASP Division, was well-known for always being dressed like a movie star. Having a nickname can also endear you to buyers and make you more unique. No one forgets nicknames like Ol' Blue Eyes or The Duke, and for you younger readers who think I'm not so hip, I do know who P Diddy is. My dad's name was Charles, but his nickname was Bud or Buddy, and that helped him be remembered by his clients and buyers.

Being unique and standing out also can be accomplished through marketing techniques like the postcards Joe Girard mailed out or the celebrity photos Chuck T. displayed in his office. I send out unusual, hand-signed thank-you cards, with a million-dollar bill enclosed, to anyone I meet personally. People have raved about receiving them and told me they were fun.

Sales pros never seem to follow a cookie-cutter approach. Most top producers I've worked with, observed, or trained created their own system for success. But they all build a Headliner reputation by figuring out how to become *the* specialist in their market niche and become unique to their buyers.

Follow these Power Boosters to turn your identity into a reputation.

POWER BOOSTERS

- Do not put money, profit, or commissions ahead of serving your buyers.

- Do what you say, when you say you'll do it—for all your buyers, all the time!

- Send unique thank-you cards to all buyers on a regular basis. These are a necessity for anyone serious about sales stardom.

- Acknowledge the business and personal successes of your buyers with a phone call, e-mail, or card.

- Remember personal stories, birthdays, etc., and bring them up in conversation to reconnect with clients. Make them feel special.

- Have a follow-up notebook/manual for the buyer after the sale. In real estate, it might be an owner's manual for their new home, or it might be a notebook describing what you'd do to market their home if they listed with you.

- Personally demonstrate your product's operation with all of the buyer's end-users yourself, after the purchase of the product— this shows your personal commitment to serving them.

- Conduct regular account reviews with all your buyers, assessing how your product or service is meeting their needs and how you might be able to provide even greater value for them.

(continued)

- Personally introduce your staff or support personnel to your buyers so they feel like family after the sale.

- Narrow your selling focus to one market niche, or maybe one product category, or one customer profile—so you can become *the* specialist.

- Join the appropriate associations for your market niche.

- Become the expert—*the* specialist—by immersing yourself in your market knowledge.

- Network yourself among business contacts within your market focus.

- Identify what makes *you* unique or unusual now, and accentuate the factors that you feel are reputation enhancers.

- Experiment with various other ways to stand out and become a Headliner in your niche.

LEVERAGE IT! USING YOUR REPUTATION TO INCREASE SALES

Sales superstars work hard to turn their credible personal identities into solid reputations that are front-and-center in the public eye, but they don't stop there. They know that they can easily leverage those reputations to send their sales soaring. They make sure that buyers form a positive impression of them before they've even met, and they accomplish this by capitalizing on both their *company's* reputation and their *personal* reputations.

Capitalize on Your Company's Reputation

In 1993, an obviously agitated surgical nursing director looked up from her desk and snarled at me with much attitude, "And who might *you* be with?"

I confidently replied, "Ma'am, I'm with Johnson & Johnson."

"You don't say! Well, go ahead and have a seat, and I'll be with you shortly," she cordially replied, before turning to bark an order at a circulating nurse.

After 13 years in sales, the power of a company's reputation didn't fully sink in until that day when I witnessed a complete attitudinal metamorphosis upon hearing the name Johnson & Johnson. A company's reputation is one of the biggest guns in a salesperson's arsenal.

As a salesperson, you must capitalize on your company's reputation to reduce buyer resistance, particularly during the early stages of the sales process. You must also minimize any negative reputation factors if they exist. Right or wrong, your buyers usually have a perception—a feeling—about your product or service, usually before you ever show up. They have been prepared—preframed—through advertising, word-of-mouth, and the media to believe certain things about your company. As we all know, sometimes these impressions are accurate, and sometimes they're not. Sometimes they help you, and sometimes they hurt you.

Preframing is simply sending communications, targeted to reach your buyers in advance of meeting, to develop a positive bias toward your company and products. Great companies have long histories of successfully preframing buyers to feel positive about their reputation. In the next section of this chapter, I'll share the strategies you can use to preframe buyers about you, establishing your personal reputation in advance and predisposing them to buy.

Every business organization should have a VP of Reputation.
—GEORGE LUDWIG

So how do you capitalize on a company's reputation? A no-brainer is to sell for a company with an outstanding reputation. Identify several of the most reputable companies in your industry and try to work for one of them. My career specialty was selling high-tech medical devices, so I'd been eyeing Johnson & Johnson for some time. When the opportunity arose for me to help them launch an exciting new division in 1993, I jumped on it. That turned out to be my best career move. Johnson & Johnson has consistently been ranked near the top of *Fortune* magazine's Most Admired Companies in America. They've won countless awards for philanthropy, being well-run, having a diverse workplace, serving clients, and being financially sound. The bottom line is, they have one of the best corporate reputations in America and have enjoyed that fine distinction since their inception in 1866. I'm not here to plug my old company, just to make the point that your company's reputation plays a huge role in your sales success.

If you talk with salespeople, or former salespeople, from Enron, World-Com, or even Martha Stewart, you'll hear the challenges, frustrations, and, in some instances, the devastation that they experienced trying to sell for a firm whose reputation was in jeopardy. So, if you can, work for one of the very best.

Second, you must be able to articulate your company's unique story and any anecdotes or testimonials that will form your company's reputation in the mind of the buyer. Northwestern Mutual, the insurance and financial giant, enjoys an elite status as one of the most admired companies in America. They even have the distinction of being identified as a company with one of the best-trained sales forces in America. Jim H., one of their top producers in Illinois, said that one strategic key to being successful in the highly competitive environment of insurance sales was to have a handy arsenal of third-party testimonials that expound upon the company's impeccable reputation. One testimonial their reps share with potential buyers is that Northwestern Mutual has been rated number one in their industry, according to *Fortune* magazine's Most Admired Companies in America, for the 20th straight time since the survey started in 1983. That's a huge credibility creator and reputation builder, and it helps buyers feel more secure about doing business with the company. It worked for me; I bought two policies!

> *In matters of style, swim with the current; in matters of principle,*
> *stand like a rock.*
> **—THOMAS JEFFERSON**

Another example of how you can capitalize on your company's reputation is a technique that Johnson & Johnson's salespeople use from time to time to showcase their credibility. The company has embraced a companywide, one-page credo since 1944, which has become legendary among both employees and outside business gurus because of its effect on the corporate culture, the firm's reputation, and, ultimately, on the millions of buyers who feel safe doing business with Johnson & Johnson.

The salespeople often share the credo with buyers and potential buyers—especially when they're competing with another firm that might be selling primarily on price because of a questionable track record or reputation. Johnson & Johnson's credo serves as the ultimate communication to buyers, employees, and investors of the integrity, values, and competence that are woven into the fabric of the organization. To see the credo, log on to http://www.jnj.com and look under the section, "Our Company."

Another way to capitalize on your company's reputation is to tell personal stories about times when the company went the extra mile for a buyer or provided a solution that made a major difference in a customer's life.

What do you do if your company has a bad reputation, or if the buyer's perception of your company's reputation is less than favorable? Jump off a cliff! (Not really—but you've gotta keep a sense of humor.)

If your company truly has a bad reputation, then you can choose one of several options. You can go sell somewhere else. This is often the wisest move. Another option is to stick around and help improve your company's reputation, especially if the condition has not been persistent or long term. You can rattle the cage with sales management, the president, or anybody who will listen, because this is serious stuff. You can't sell successfully for the long haul with a company that is not committed to having a solid reputation. If no one listens, move on.

If the buyer's perception is wrong and your company truly has a fine reputation, then use the questioning and listening techniques detailed in Chapter 3 to position their concern in the most favorable light for continuing the sales process.

The last technique for overcoming a less-than-stellar company reputation is to leverage your personal reputation in such a way that you're perceived as being more important in the buying process than the company. You'll see how that's done in the next section.

Leverage Your Personal Reputation

People buy from people. People buy from people they trust. No matter what your company's reputation is, ultimately your reputation determines whether they'll buy from you. But if you want to become one of the selling elite, you have to make sure potential buyers experience your reputation firsthand.

The challenge is this: you can be competent, confident, committed, and have impeccable character. You can have a positive image, be focused on serving, be *the* specialist, and be unique. But you still won't enjoy the benefits of the Power of Reputation to turbocharge your sales results until you get the word out to potential buyers.

You must preframe buyers by promoting your reputation and identity so that buyers seek *you* out instead of you seeking them out. Preframing is marketing you to your clients and potential buyers in a way that predisposes them to buy from you. Your efforts get multiplied, because you reach a far greater number of people than you could by knocking on their doors one at a time. In addition, the people who seek you out will already have their trust meter out of the suspicious range.

The Swiss engineer, Alfred Büchi, first had the idea of using the exhaust energy of a reciprocating engine for direct propulsion purposes. He invented the turbocharger that Porsche would finally make famous 70 years later. (I told you I was obsessed with Porsches.) The turbocharger's brilliance is simply using what you already have in a way that creates exponentially greater results. Preframing potential buyers through personal marketing does the same thing—it uses the reputation you already have to turbocharge your sales results like nothing else can.

Now, you may think I have lost it when I tell you that one of the keys to becoming a sales superstar is to stop thinking like a salesperson— you've got to think like a marketer, too. You're a salesperson first, but you're a *personal marketer* second. I've experienced this in my own sales career with amazing results.

When I joined Johnson & Johnson in 1993, the Advanced Sterilization Products division was so new, we didn't even have brochures about our revolutionary new sterilization process to show hospital personnel. Because I was new to sterilization decision makers but enjoyed a strong reputation in Chicago hospitals, I decided to try some personal marketing to augment my selling efforts. I had never done anything but sell, sell, and sell. But after reading Dr. Robert Cialdini's book, *Influence: The Psychology of Persuasion,* I had become convinced that the world's most powerful persuaders use a combination of both selling and marketing tactics.

I tested his theory by doing a series of three mailings to approximately 200 sterilization decision makers. The first was a letter introducing me, the new process, and my desire to share it with them—no strings attached. The second mailing was a testimonial letter from a California hospital that had been a beta site for the technology. And the third letter, which took a great deal of time, showcased an attached, highlighted article from one of the journals on sterilization. It also included a handwritten note from me in the letter's margin about a particular reference who knew me from his hospital.

The results were convincing. I'd always been a guy who set up every sales appointment by making dozens of calls to the same potential buyer until they finally relented. I've even been accused of trying to climb through the phone to get an appointment! But here's what happened—from those 600 letters (200 decision makers × 3 mailings) came 26 return calls requesting an appointment. I was excited . . . they were calling *me* . . . what a kick! From those 26 appointments, 12 hospitals indicated they were interested in pursuing a full investigation with a potential purchase within one calendar year. From those 12, 7 purchased that year, bringing in more than $700,000 in business and helping me win a Glamour Trip and take the stage for a national sales award. Time to party!

Dan Kennedy, one of the nation's top marketing gurus and author of several books on the subject, says, "Try not to talk with anyone who doesn't already know you." The more potential buyers call you, the less effort you have to expend to cold call new business, the number-one dreaded activity of all salespeople, from rookies to masters. The more quality effort you put into *marketing* you, the less you have to physically *sell* you. Remember: This personal marketing is separate from the global marketing your company is already doing for you. This is personalized promotion designed to pique potential buyers' interest in *you* and your product or service.

> *If you do what you have always done,*
> *you will get what you have always gotten.*
> **—ANONYMOUS**

So how do you market your reputation to preframe your buyers? Three simple methods are *advance marketing, personal contact marketing,* and *Headliner marketing.* Most sales superstars use the first two heavily, but the third, while being the most ambiguous and long term, offers the greatest possible leverage.

Advance marketing. This type of marketing involves no direct physical contact with the buyer. It includes e-mail marketing, e-zine newsletters, direct mail promotions, newsletters, sales letters, faxes, and advertising. All of these marketing tactics will get your name in front of buyers before they meet you, but they can also be used during the sales process. They range from being very expensive—advertising, for example—to being very inexpensive—e-mailing your buyers information of value.

Coca-Cola, Nike, and all great advertisers know that buyers need to see a name at least six times before they'll remember it. Your buyers are no different. The more they recognize you, the greater the likelihood that they'll trust you. Advance marketing should be an ongoing commitment to keep your name out there in your niche, both to draw in new business and to keep you in front of current clients in a hypercompetitive economy. Don't count on your company, either; your only guarantee for becoming a sales master is in what *you* do.

Creating a powerful sales letter or fax, like I used at Johnson & Johnson, is a valuable tool—especially if you call on high-level decision makers. Anthony Parinello, author of *Selling to VITO: The Very Important Top Officer,* shares some excellent tips on how to construct those letters, but nothing is more important than to make sure your letter, or fax, stands out from the deluge of mail and to show that you've targeted a very specific audience and done your homework. Following up sales letters or faxes with phone calls also dramatically increases your success ratio.

You can make your advance marketing efforts more effective by following a few easy tips. First, do your homework on your targeted audience prior to sending anything out. Make sure your target list is well defined and truly bona fide. Next, have a single, clear-cut objective for your fax, e-mail, or sales letter. Then, remember that quality is king and that your communication must be unique to stand out. Finally, you must commit to frequent communications, not a one-time campaign, if you want real results.

My sales letter campaign in 1993 for Johnson & Johnson convinced me of the power of advance marketing. In my career as an author, speaker, and consultant, it has proven itself many times over. Press notices announcing the release of my first book, *Wise Moves,* landed me countless radio and newspaper interviews. My e-magazine, *Brain Bytes,* has generated numerous speaking engagements and significant book sales. I hope you're as sold as I am on using advance marketing as a turbocharger to leverage your reputation.

Personal contact marketing. This type of marketing involves either in-person contact with your buyers or telephone contact. It includes referrals and testimonials, networking, customer site visits, customer seminars, and association involvement. Referrals are the single most valuable form of marketing you can use. They constitute what Dr. Robert Cialdini calls Social Proof. It simply means that what a buyer determines to be correct is based partly on what other people think is correct. Buyers are more likely to buy if they see others buying, especially those they trust.

Referrals and testimonials are critical to becoming a sales superstar. Satisfied, loyal clients (you do have at least one, don't you?) who speak to other potential buyers and who make an introduction that includes a personal endorsement about *you* (not just your product or service) spread your reputation like wildfire. "Bob's a good guy." "Debbie will treat you right." "You can totally trust Jerry."

These simple introductions give you credibility and respect that would otherwise take a long time to develop. The higher the level of decision maker to whom you're trying to sell, the more critical these introductions become. Rick Page, author of *Hope Is Not a Strategy*, describes it this way:

> The best way to get access to an executive is through another executive or trusted colleague. Executives are barraged every day with dozens of voice mails, e-mails, and phone messages. Many of these are nonbusiness calls or not important. However, the ones that get the most attention and credibility are the ones they are expecting based on the recommendation of a colleague. I call it "transferred trust" or "the friend of my friend is my friend."

So what's the best way to secure referrals and testimonials? First, keep reminding your satisfied clients that an introduction to another potential buyer would be of great value. Second, begin building what's known as an *advocate list*. This is a list of 25 to 40 clients, contacts, and friends who you believe will refer you to the most new sales opportunities. Commit to stay in touch with your advocates at least once a month. Try to add value for them and their businesses—remember to focus on serving. Maybe a referral or two for them would be the ticket. Your clients who provide you with a successful referral should receive a tangible reward. Send them a book, tickets to a game; go to lunch, or at least send a thank-you card. As you regularly monitor your list, you'll discover that some of the people you originally thought would be your best advocates are not. Keep those folks as friends or clients, but remove them from your advocacy list. Prune this list every three months.

You must also work hard to collect letters from satisfied buyers who will tout *you* and your products or services. Work to secure big-name testimonials to add credibility. Remember how Chuck T. used all his satisfied celebrity clients to give him an edge? Buyers will figure that if a sports star will work with him, why shouldn't *they* work with him, too?

Another key to personal contact marketing is simply getting in front of potential buyers in a nonselling environment. Host educational seminars for potential buyers, join and attend association meetings, take potential buyers to visit satisfied clients at their location. Do anything that helps you rub shoulders with buyers, and always strive to be seen as the specialist in those settings.

> *A wise man knows everything, a shrewd man knows everyone.*
> **—CHINESE PROVERB**

The average person knows 250 people. Those 250 also know 250, meaning that 62,500 people know your immediate contacts. That represents a huge gold mine of opportunity, no matter what you sell. Networking is *the* shovel that can dig up the gold in your Rolodex. Somebody, who knows somebody, who knows you, can help you make a sale *today*.

In the late 1960s, Stanley Milgram's research uncovered how closely humans are linked together. From that research emerged the concept of six degrees of separation, which argues that all of us, through our social networks, are within just six connections to anyone on the planet. All the top sales pros I know have big, bulging Rolodexes, because they know that's where the money is. Commit to networking and build your Rolodex every week. It's who you know, who they know, and who knows you that will get your reputation in front of every potential buyer. The salesperson with the largest Rolodex wins!

Headliner marketing. This type of marketing, which will preframe buyers to trust you and buy from you, includes public speaking, writing articles, and obtaining publicity. Headliner marketing thrusts you into the limelight as the specialist. Now, I'm reading your mind, and you're thinking, "C'mon, I'm just in sales. What's all the rigamarole about speaking and stuff?" Let me show you.

Julie P., a Century 21 sales associate, speaks at chamber of commerce luncheons and service organizations in her area. She gives a talk titled, "The Seven Deadliest Mistakes New Home Buyers Make." Julie gives her presentation *pro bono,* but because community members learn from her expertise, they send lots of referrals her way. Tim K. submitted an article to one of the trade journals in the hospitality industry about tips for selecting a meeting location. That exposure helped him book many meetings for the resort properties he represented, and he reprinted it to use as a marketing collateral piece. Tim is on his way to becoming a Headliner.

During my medical sales days, I once had the opportunity to present an inspirational message to a national nursing association's annual convention and got exposure to 4,000 nurse buyers at one time. That one talk opened a *ton* of doors for new business. It didn't hurt my dating calendar, either! The more people who see you as the expert, the more they'll trust you and want to buy from you.

While salespeople use this type of marketing the least, because it requires bold action with a very uncertain payoff, this method has the most leverage. It's the most leveraged form of marketing because it reaches the largest number of potential buyers in each effort or campaign. And, when it does work, the payoff is huge.

Let's wrap up this chapter with the Power Boosters to leverage your reputation for increased sales.

POWER BOOSTERS

- Make an honest assessment of your company's reputation.

- Work for a company with an outstanding reputation or at least a firm that's committed to building one.

- Make sure that your company provides reputation-enhancing printed materials.

(continued)

- Articulate your company's story as it relates to credibility and reputation when appropriate with buyers.

- Secure and share with buyers third-party testimonials about your company's reputation.

- Have several personal stories where your company's reputation and credibility shined for a buyer.

- Commit to doing at least one form of advance marketing: a sales letter or fax campaign, e-zine, direct mail, etc.

- Develop your advocacy list of at least 25 people who will provide you referrals.

- Commit to call your best clients and secure a referral or at least a testimonial.

- Join an association that represents the buyers in your niche.

- Try taking buyers to a satisfied buyer's location, or organize a buyer's educational seminar.

- Commit to build your Rolodex and mine the gold from your network.

LET'S RECAP

I hope you're as convinced as I am that nothing is more important in the world of sales than reputation. Remember how astounded John G. was when someone was willing to spend $55,000 without even meeting him—because of his outstanding reputation? That's how the selling elite get business!

Buyers are more suspicious than ever today, and the Power of Reputation is the strongest antidote you have for combating it. Commit to building a great personal identity. Take inventory of who you are, believe with all your heart that you can become better, and use the C-CORE to make sure you're credible and trustworthy.

Turn your identity into a well-known reputation by remembering to provide the best service possible to your buyers. Make sure you're a Headliner in their news by standing out as unique and as an expert in your niche.

Then you can put it all together to explode your sales by leveraging your company's reputation as well as your own, hard-earned reputation. Preframe your buyers to buy from *you* with the techniques of advance marketing, personal contact marketing, and Headliner marketing.

Reputation resides in every sales superstar's DNA. But unlike genetics, which cannot be legally altered, a salesperson's DNA can be changed. It's mighty hard work, but if you commit to improving, you'll be rewarded with a lasting return on your investment.

The ancient Romans were noted for their achievements in construction. Many Roman arches are still standing. They've survived for more than 2,000 years.

The Romans had an interesting practice. When they finished building an arch, the engineer in charge was expected to stand beneath it when the scaffolding was removed.

If the arch didn't hold, he was the first to know.

However you choose to build your reputation, build it so that you—and someday your children's children—can stand beneath it with confidence and pride.

2

THE POWER OF
REAL PASSION

Enter the Supercharged Selling State

The most powerful weapon on earth is the human soul on fire.
—MARSHALL FERDINAND FOCH

I was ten years old, wearing only underwear like crazy kids often do, playing Ping Pong against my friend Ralph in the cool, unfinished basement of our Indiana home on a hot, sticky August afternoon. After beating Ralph over 40 straight games, I felt invincible. I was in such a confident state that I literally could not miss a shot.

I was spinning the ball, slamming the ball, pulling shots out of nowhere. I had a grin on my face that was a mile wide and would not leave. Time seemed to stand still. I managed to win eight more matches before Ralph left . . . dejected, depressed, and downtrodden. This was my earliest memory of being in the state of peak performance, that state of unstoppable passion.

I was the real-life "Captain Underpants," minus the cape. For years I thought wearing only underwear was the best way to perform at a peak level—until I finally realized that outer clothing produced great results, too! I also discovered, 20 years later, that the peak state I had accessed while playing Ping Pong against Ralph was the most resourceful emotional state for selling and that the Power of Real Passion can boost sales success instantaneously. It's part of a sales superstar's DNA, because it puts both the salesperson and the buyer in the optimal state for selling and buying. I still recommend underwear for everybody but for different reasons, and, amazingly, Ralph remained my friend—and never even required therapy!

Can you remember a time like that when you were on a major roll, totally in *the zone*, doing things almost flawlessly? Maybe it was a round of golf, a business meeting, or playing the piano. You hit the ball consistently right down the middle of the fairway, or you problem-solved a thorny business dilemma right off the top of your head. I bet you can also remember experiencing the very opposite effect, too—when everything you did went wrong. Every golf shot headed straight for the rough, you went blank in the middle of a corporate presentation, and whatever you touched seemed to turn to crapola.

What causes these differences in your behavior? You're the same person in both scenarios. Why can an athlete hit every shot one day and then can't buy one the next? The difference is simply what state you're in. And I do not mean Indiana, New York, or California! I mean the psychoneuro-physiological state you happen to be accessing at any given time.

Most people label these mental-emotional-physical states as simply emotions or states of mind. Anthony Robbins, a leading peak performance expert and author of *Unlimited Power,* describes *state* as the sum total of millions of neurological processes happening within us, combined with the sum total of our experience, at any given moment in time. These emotions, or states, that we experience are literally biochemical bursts in our brains and bodies. Mind and body are completely interconnected, so that your thoughts immediately influence your physiology and vice versa.

There are the positive states—such as confidence, love, compassion, happiness, strength, ecstasy, certainty, and passion. Positive states maximize the use of the mind and physiology to ensure better feelings and improved performance. The ultimate positive state of mind, the peak performance state, has empowered people to break boards with their bare hands, walk across 1200-degree coals, or lie on a bed of nails without the slightest injury. It's where your mind, your energy, and your confidence are at their highest levels. There are also the negative states—like anger, weakness, depression, hate, frustration, confusion, loneliness, boredom, tentativeness, and insecurity—and they lead to weakened performance. Stay away from these negative states for selling.

Just like athletes, sales superstars know that their sales success is not so much a reflection of their abilities but rather a result of which state of mind they consistently live in, especially when they're with buyers. They know that the peak performance state, that state of unstoppable passion, is the *supercharged selling state.* The Power of Real Passion declares that by improving your state, you will dramatically improve your selling effectiveness. By entering the right emotional state—the supercharged selling state—you're more creative, confident, resourceful, competent, certain, and passionate about selling and serving your buyer. Remember *selling is serving?*

The world's greatest salespeople take control of their emotional states no matter what the external circumstances. They sell circles around the average salesperson by refusing to slip into a disempowering state, even when confronted with negative circumstances or buyers. Our ability to exist in the supercharged selling state also transfers to the buyer. Selling is nothing more than the transference of your energy and emotion—*your state*—from you to your buyer.

I am so passionate about this concept that I am going to make a bold statement: buyers do *not* buy products, services, or ideas; they *buy states.*

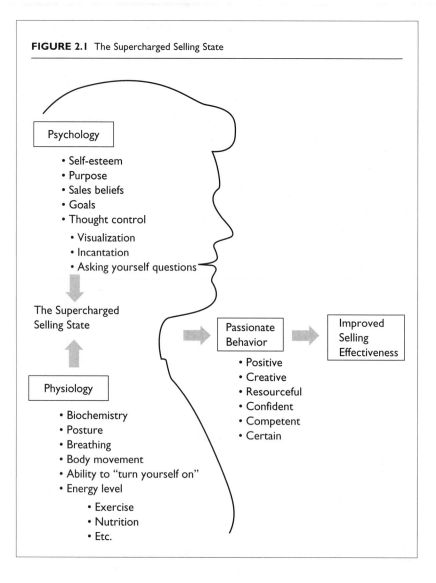

FIGURE 2.1 The Supercharged Selling State

Psychology

- Self-esteem
- Purpose
- Sales beliefs
- Goals
- Thought control
  - Visualization
  - Incantation
  - Asking yourself questions

The Supercharged
Selling State

Physiology

- Biochemistry
- Posture
- Breathing
- Body movement
- Ability to "turn yourself on"
- Energy level
  - Exercise
  - Nutrition
  - Etc.

Passionate
Behavior

- Positive
- Creative
- Resourceful
- Confident
- Competent
- Certain

Improved
Selling
Effectiveness

They buy the emotional state that they associate with you, your product, or your service. They buy the products or services that they imagine will provide them with their most desired *feelings*. A buyer's willingness to purchase at any given point in time is a result of the state of mind they're in. Thus, sales superstars know they're more than just salespeople—they are really state prompters. Top producers know that to influence a buyer, they must prompt or induce a very positive state and then anchor that positive state of mind to the product or service they're selling. Conversely, a negative state can also transfer to the buyer through body language, voice inflections, or word choices and result in the loss of a sale.

I frequently ask salespeople in my training seminars what they sell. I hear responses like *office furniture, real estate, cars, financial services, pharmaceuticals, insurance, productivity enhancement,* and the ever-popular *myself.* (I think this is illegal in most states in the USA.) Put this thinking aside. If you don't realize what you're really selling, you can't become a sales master.

Gary L., a sales manager for a large real estate broker, recently had his team trained in this concept. They began to realize, "We don't sell homes. We sell *feelings*—we sell *states.* We sell comfort. We sell safety. We sell security. We sell value. We sell peace of mind. We sell lifestyle." According to Gary, this breakthrough realization—that they actually sold emotional states—helped them to increase their home sales significantly.

The DNA of sales superstars includes the Power of Real Passion, which teaches them how to operate from the supercharged selling state. Supercharging is the technology of supplying air to an internal-combustion engine at greater than atmospheric pressure. The result is an abundance of energy and power. Just like a high-performance automobile, your "sales machine" operates best when it's fueled by the supercharged selling state. Your abundance of confidence, competence, and energy ignites into an unstoppable passion that shifts a buyer's perceptions, feelings, and actions toward purchasing your product. Sales superstars know that the secret to having plenty of this fuel is to be able to change their psychological focus and physiology at will. In other words, they *supercharge their psychology, supercharge their physiology,* and then *apply that supercharged state* to sales.

SUPERCHARGE YOUR PSYCHOLOGY

Only passions, great passions, can elevate the soul to great things.
—DENIS DIDEROT

Todd B., a medical-device salesperson, had been through a horrible quarter and was on the verge of being fired. When the new quarter began, he couldn't stop focusing on last quarter's disappointing results every day. This put Todd in an unresourceful, negative, and depressing state, often before his sales calls. It felt like his emotions were out of his control. Zig Ziglar, one of my first sales mentors, would have simply said, "Todd, you got a case of 'stinking thinking.'" Fortunately for Todd, he learned how to supercharge his psychology and turned his situation around. He did it by developing a sound psychological foundation, establishing clear goals, and directing his thoughts in a productive way.

Start with Your Psychological Foundation

Supercharging your psychology is primarily a matter of controlling your mental focus during the hours you're selling, especially when you're with your buyers. Before you can take charge of your mental focus, however, you must have a solid psychological foundation. This foundation is like the filter through which the rest of your fuel runs—if it's clogged up with negative attitudes and perceptions, none of your sales behaviors and efforts will run efficiently. Three factors—your *self-esteem,* your *purpose,* and your *sales beliefs*—make up the psychological foundation needed to control your mental focus.

Self-esteem. Your psychological foundation starts with self-esteem, the beliefs you have about yourself and what you're capable of. How you see yourself will greatly influence your mental focus and your ability to get into a positive state. If you see yourself as a phenomenal salesperson with a great future ahead, it's much easier to get excited and energized about your selling. Because Todd B. didn't see himself as capable of great success, he could only focus on how poorly he had performed the previous quarter.

The good news is that, if your self-esteem is not at the level you want it to be, it can be improved. Remember your personal identity from Chapter 1. The work you put in on building that identity and developing your C-CORE (competence, confidence, commitment, and character) will also raise your self-esteem. *Decide* that you're already a great salesperson and that you'll pay the necessary price to become even greater. Salespeople who feel good about themselves sell more. You will not become a sales superstar if you don't feel *damn good* about yourself, period. Improve the efficiency of your psychological "fuel filter" by committing to build your self-esteem.

Purpose. A well-defined sense of purpose is the second component of your psychological foundation. It gives you the personal power to call forth the positive, passionate mental focus needed to enter the supercharged selling state consistently and sell at the top. In my 25 years selling, training, and coaching salespeople, I've noticed that very few salespeople have a defined purpose for their careers. They don't know why they do what they do. Most salespeople remain unsatisfied and inconsistent in their sales results, because they don't have that deep inner drive that fuels their psychology every day.

Salespeople are notoriously gung ho when they first get hired. They're highly motivated self-starters, very driven to sell. But as time wears on and market conditions shift, their excitement wanes and they get bored. Then they usually move on somewhere else, only to repeat the cycle all over again a few years later. They're disconnected from their purpose—they either don't know or have lost sight of *why* they're selling in the first place. Only the sales superstars know how to end the "sales boredom circuit" by developing a well-defined life purpose.

> *Success means living the life of the heart.*
> **—FRANCIS FORD COPPOLA**

Ultimately, your sense of purpose comes down to whom you want to become and what you want to achieve. How do you define success? What's driving you? You must probe deep to uncover your purpose. Most salespeople in my seminars tell me that they're driven by either money or recognition. While these both are big drivers for sales superstars, usually a deeper purpose lies underneath.

Carol R., an advertising salesperson, told me that she was driven by money. When I asked her why, she said that money represented freedom for her and more time with her family. Probing deeper, we discovered that more time really represented the ability for her to make a bigger difference in her children's lives and in her philanthropic efforts at church. After a few months of reflecting on what motivates her, she realized that her real purpose was to "make a difference in everyone's life," including the buyers she called upon every day. As result of her discovery, Carol now spends every single sales day focusing her mental thoughts on making a difference in people's lives. Her clear purpose propels her into the supercharged selling state. She is totally fired up about being in sales and has become her company's top producer. When salespeople recognize their deepest drive and purpose, they create a psychological power base that allows them to control their mental focus and increase their sales.

Sales beliefs. The third factor that makes up your psychological "fuel filter" is your beliefs, specifically those that apply to sales. The study of beliefs and belief systems became enormously popular when Richard Bandler and John Grinder introduced the science of neurolinguistic programming to the world in the early 1970s. Grinder, a linguistics professor at Stanford University, and Bandler, a psychology student interested in psychotherapy, teamed to study the patterns of the world's leading therapists. They never intended to found a school of therapy, but that's ultimately what happened. Peak performance expert Anthony Robbins, who helped the science become popular, brilliantly simplified their theories, so that the everyday person could apply them to achieve greater success. I encourage you to read any of the books written by Bandler and Grinder or the popular tomes by Mr. Robbins. This science is *very* powerful stuff.

> *They can because they think they can.*
> **—VERGIL**

What does all this have to do with selling? Quite a bit, actually. *Beliefs* are the ideas that you think are true, and Bandler and Grinder's work, as well as that of others, confirmed scientifically that you base your daily actions upon those beliefs. Beliefs control your decisions and influence the way you think and feel during every moment you're selling. They determine what you will and will not do. When you believe something, you give your mind an unquestioned command to respond in a certain way. A positive set of beliefs makes it easier to shape your psychological focus and enter the supercharged selling state.

Sally P., a veteran salesperson in the financial services industry, had the *belief* that answering machines and voice mail were to be avoided at all costs. She even bragged to fellow salespeople that she had been able to set appointments for 11 years without ever leaving an electronic message. When she attended our sales training segment for prospecting by phone, she began to realize that perhaps she should rethink her approach. Her ability to reach decision makers had declined recently, because they all seemed to be so much busier these days. In fact, her sales results were at an all-time low. After hearing about our prospecting formula, she wondered if her belief had limited her ability to leave effective messages. She realized that her aversion to leaving recorded communication cut her off from the chance to leave messages that were powerful and provocative. Her decision to *start believing* that electronic messages were useful tools led to increased access to decision makers and better sales results.

Sales superstars figure out which beliefs—for their particular makeup, situation, and industry—will enable them to sell like a runaway train. You must do the same. But most of the top producers seem to share a set of general beliefs, and I encourage you to model them. Try to "step into" this belief system—if someone else can do it, you can do it. Try on these sales beliefs of the selling elite.

- Past sales do not equal future sales.
- There is no sales failure; there is only feedback to perform better.
- There is always a way to turn sales around, if I'm committed.
- There is a solution to every problem I encounter.
- For sales to get better, I must get better.

Top sales achievers also develop enabling beliefs about all aspects of their selling expertise, the sales process, their products, and their company. Each of those beliefs builds up their psychological foundation and gives them easier access to the peak performance state where they can outsell their competitors.

Focus on Your Goals

Laying a good foundation is only the first step in supercharging your psychology to enter the ideal selling state. Controlling your mental focus also involves setting clear and ambitious goals. Goals are the secret genie to sales success. Remember Aladdin's lamp from the Arabian tales— *The Thousand and One Nights?* Goal setting has such a powerful effect on your mental focus that it's like having your own personal genie with un-limited wishes. *When you focus on your goals, your goals focus you on success.*

The world's greatest sales achievers often begin with the very same first step: setting a goal. Mark Victor Hansen—who is one of America's most sought-after sales trainers, speakers, and authors—knows how to sell in a big way. He and his partner, Jack Canfield, have sold more than 90 million copies of their Chicken Soup for the Soul series, making it one of the best-selling nonfiction book series in history. Mark told me that the number-one factor, aside from his spiritual convictions, that led to his phenomenal success has been the fact that he sets a ton of goals. He also sets BIG goals. His current goal is to sell one billion books by 2020 and raise $500 million for charity by the same date. Now *that* is a megagoal!

> *We all have two choices: we can make a living or we can design a life.*
> **—JIM ROHN**

Goals keep the top sales producers' mental focus where it should be—even when they're afraid or things aren't going well. They can bounce back, because their goals create a compelling future, a future worth fighting for. Goals can create such a powerful psychological focus that you become unstoppable in their pursuit. Clearly written goals concentrate your personal power, and they unlock your positive thoughts and energy. Goals intensify your belief that success is possible for you, and they help you make better decisions and choices.

Whatever you dwell upon in your mind grows and expands in your reality. What do the selling elite dwell upon? Their goals—and you can, too. Just like Mark Victor Hansen, the more you think about your goals, the more you'll make them a reality. Brian Tracy, author of *Advanced Selling Strategies*, shares an interesting quip about Sir Isaac Newton being asked how he had managed to make such a great contribution to the field of physics in his lifetime. Sir Isaac Newton responded, "By thinking of nothing else."

> *There is a law in psychology that if you form a picture in your mind of what you would like to be, and you keep and hold that picture there long enough, you will soon become exactly as you had been thinking.*
> **—WILLIAM JAMES**

Goals have immense power on your psychology because they activate a mechanism in your brain known as the reticular activating system (RAS), which determines what your brain focuses on at any given time. Because an enormous number of stimuli is bombarding your brain all the time, it needs to decide what to include in and what to delete from your conscious awareness. The RAS is the screening device of the brain. It directs your focus to what's important to you, and creating specific goals puts your sales on the "important" list.

Have you ever bought a new car that you thought was not totally "mainstream" yet? You patted yourself on the back, convinced you were finally on the cutting edge, setting the trend. Then, right after you got the vehicle, you began to see them everywhere, like they were coming out of the woodwork. The RAS mechanism of your brain now picked out your car model from the zillions of others on the road and put your mental focus on it. Those cars had always been there, but you hadn't noticed. This shift in your mental focus is exactly what happens when the RAS becomes directed by your goals. By making something a priority in your life through setting it as a goal, you create the emotional intensity and conviction to eventually attain it.

We grow through dreams. All great men and women are dreamers.
Some, however, allow their dreams to die. You should nurse your dreams
and protect them through bad times and tough times to the sunshine
and light which always come.
—WOODROW WILSON

In 1979, I first experienced the awesome power that goals have to change your life. After listening to motivational icon Zig Ziglar, I became convinced that I needed to set goals in every area of my life. I set my first goals in the Mr. Donut coffee shop on State Street, in Fort Wayne, Indiana, my home town. (I didn't have too many health and fitness goals prior to that day.) I wrote down every possible thing I ever hoped of being, doing, having, creating, experiencing, and contributing. I wrote for four-and-a-half straight hours—boy, was I wired on all the coffee and glazed donuts! The timeline I established for accomplishing those goals was anywhere from one month to making it into heaven 75 years later. I wrote down everything without thinking how I would accomplish it. I pretended that I was a kid writing down his Christmas wish list.

How powerful have those goals been for me? When being interviewed for a newspaper article about my first book, *Wise Moves,* I pulled out my very first goal list. Those goals had a powerful effect in transforming my life, propelling me to an amazing level of success. At the time, I had no idea how the dreams that I had written down as goals could ever be pulled off. I just trusted in the power of goals to transform those dreams into reality, the process by which Zig swore. My very first goal list had dreams of becoming a sales superstar, becoming a pilot, running a marathon, designing a sportswear line (http://www.urbanwarriorsportswear .com), writing a book, becoming a speaker or performer, inspiring people to overcome adversity, following my Creator, enjoying financial abundance, living on the waterfront, learning to water-ski, owning a Porsche 911, seeing Rio de Janeiro and the French Riviera, and countless other goals. Amazingly, all of these have already come true, and more than 80 percent of all the goals I wrote down in 1979 have been achieved.

While you never reach all your goals, the very act of setting them shifts your psychological focus and will ultimately shift your destiny. Since that day in 1979, I've continued to set bigger and bigger goals, including making this book one of the best-written and best-selling sales books of all time. Know anyone who could use a copy? (See? My goals constantly shape what occupies my attention.)

The world's greatest salespeople all use goals to shape their mental focus and enter the supercharged selling state. They also know that their goals must be written down and reviewed consistently. Writing your goals downloads them into the RAS of the brain, and reviewing them regularly activates the subconscious mind to work on them. To harness this power, you'll need sales goals, income goals, client-builder goals, and many others. Remember that your life in sales or business is *your* story, and the power of your goals enables you to write the ending you want. Simply write down what you would go after if you knew you could not fail. Go to a donut shop if you have to, like I did, but put yourself in the mindset of a child; ask for anything and everything—without fear of failure or rejection. These goals will supercharge your psychology and ignite your passion.

- I am earning $_____ this year.
- I am going to win the _____ sales award this year.
- I am improving my C-CORE by _____.

- I am at my ideal weight of _____ pounds.
- To become healthy and fit, I'm _____.
- My spiritual growth will include _____.
- I am developing the new sales habit of _____.
- I am dumping the bad sales habit of _____.
- My additional sales education will include _____.
- I am in possession of a brand new _____ automobile.
- My dream house can be described as _____.
- I will have $1 million net worth by _____.
- Other dreams: _____.

Direct Your Thoughts

The final step in controlling your mental focus to enter the supercharged selling state is to direct your thoughts. A surprisingly large amount of time is spent doing activities that don't require any real *thought*. Habits and social roles and routine aspects of your job control a large part of daily life. Functioning on "auto pilot" may make your day go smoothly, but when it comes to sales, it won't give you the mental sharpness that you need to be effective. You can take control of your mental processes and perform at peak levels by practicing these three techniques: *visualization, incantation,* and *asking questions.*

Visualization. One of the most effective ways to direct your thoughts and control your mental focus is visualization—playing out some sequence of events as a mental movie. Jerome Singer, the Yale psychologist who has studied mental imagery perhaps more than any other scientist, has shown that adults (especially salespeople) who picture their goals and rehearse situations mentally increase their chances of successful outcomes.

Visualization works best when the mental image is maintained long enough to evoke an emotional response. The emotion then creates conviction, and that conviction supercharges your state. The most effective images are also experiential. They need to have movement, like a movie, instead of being static, like a photograph. You have to see yourself being, doing, and having, or you won't get the state change.

Visualization is simply playing the game before the game. In his book, *Golf My Way,* PGA legend Jack Nicklaus described how he used this technique to become one the greats of the game. Before every shot, Jack played a mental film of the complete golf shot in his head.

> I never hit a shot, even in practice, without having a very sharp, in-focus picture in my head. It's like a color movie. First I "see" the ball where I want it to finish, nice and white and sitting up high on the bright green grass. Then the scene quickly changes and I "see" the ball going there: its path, trajectory, and shape, even its behavior on landing. Then there's a sort of fade-out, and the next scene shows me making the kind of swing that will turn the previous images into reality.

To become a sales superstar, you've got to become the next Steven Spielberg in your own mind and direct several award-winning (mental) movie productions. First, create a climactic scene for a movie that stars you walking down the red carpet to claim your "Sales Oscar" award at year-end. You'll also need a film where you see yourself driving a beautiful new sports car, or moving into your dream house, or achieving whatever goals really excite you.

You absolutely must direct a short film to use before every sales presentation, especially the important ones. Salespeople from Northwestern Mutual have been instructed by their in-house trainers to run a five-minute movie in their minds right before every presentation. They're taught first to put themselves in their favorite surroundings and then see themselves step right into a scene where they're successfully helping the potential buyer make a smart decision and buy.

Remember Todd B.? He started each day visualizing his two big sales successes to date and then substituted each potential new buyer as a "stand-in" for the original client who bought. This new mental imagery helped Todd turn around his psychology and say goodbye to "stinking thinking."

The key is to create a movie that symbolizes what you *really* want—your goal—and to run that movie in your head so many times with such emotional intensity that it becomes part and parcel of who you are and how you see yourself. Eventually, you'll unconsciously strive to make that movie come to life.

When I knew I was going to speak to a group of more than 4,000 people for the first time, I developed and played—16 times in the 8 days before the presentation—a vivid movie of me on the stage with the audience becoming very inspired and learning something of value. I saw every detail of the lights, their faces smiling and laughing, and the energy of their enjoyment. I even visualized their giving me a standing ovation at the end. Guess what? That's exactly what played out.

The key to successful visualization is to practice it frequently and with great detail. Choose a dream, goal, or result that you want to happen. Picture yourself all the way to your successful outcome, and "enjoy the show"!

Incantation. Another great tool for controlling mental focus is the repetition of positive statements to yourself until they become you. These are called *affirmations,* and they act to crowd out *negative* thoughts and self-talk. Incantation is repeating affirmations aloud with a lot of emotional intensity. Emile Coué, the French psychologist, wrote these simple words: "Every day in every way, I'm getting better and better." His belief was that anyone who repeated that phrase 100 times a day would experience great benefit. Modern medicine has proved his theory true. Patients who are ill and have repeated these words over and over with strong emotional conviction have been able to conquer their illnesses with statistically significant frequency.

I first discovered how powerful incantation can be when I attended Anthony Robbins's fire-walk experience. I and 1,500 other crazies strutted across 1,200-degree burning coals in our bare feet. Part of our preparation was to loudly yell emotionally charged affirmations. I remember one that we chanted was, "Cool moss! Cool moss! Cool moss!" to our own amazement as we confidently strolled across the hot embers. Being a Chicago Bears fan, I know that the same technique helped middle linebackers Dick Butkus and Mike Singletary fire up themselves and their teammates right before a key play.

I now use this technique in my own seminars, where we get salespeople to break boards with their bare hands. This experience shows them how to anchor the state of unstoppable passion that's needed to break through any fears or challenges that they may have in the pursuit of sales stardom. It's very effective, because 90 percent of audience members we poll doubt they can do it and are even afraid of trying it. By accomplishing something they doubted they could do, they learn how important their state is to success. We have them yelling, "I am ready, I am hungry, I am bold! I am breaking the board! I am beating my fear! I am reaching my sales goals! I am powerful!" as the music blasts and the energy builds toward the intensity of a scene at a Notre Dame football team's locker room at half-time when they're losing to Purdue.

Research shows that you forget 90 percent of everything you hear within 24 hours. But if you develop an affirmation based on what you want to change and repeat it 50 to 100 times daily, it will become engrained in your consciousness. Choose a specific belief or characteristic you feel you must change or adopt to become a sales superstar and repeat it aloud for five to ten minutes a day with heartfelt conviction. Or read the purpose statement you developed and the goals you just jotted down. You did write them down, didn't you? The impact of positive affirmations on your psychology will be astonishing. Follow these guidelines for constructing them.

- They are stated in the positive.
- They are in the present tense.
- They are short.
- They are action oriented.
- They are emotionally charged.
- They usually start with I am.
- They are related to or are your goals.

I read my top goals, my daily incantation sheet, and my yearly purpose statement aloud most mornings during the course of every week. (See Appendix A.) Family members and guests in adjacent hotel rooms will definitely think you've flipped, but they'll be copying you after your company calls your name for the Glamour Trip, sales award, and megabonus check. When incantation is combined with visualization, they become a one-two punch for directing your thoughts and supercharging your psychological state.

The important thing is to not stop questioning.
—ALBERT EINSTEIN

Asking questions. Questions and salespeople go together like butter goes with sweet corn on the cob. (You can tell I'm from Indiana.) Everyone knows that the mastery of asking questions is a trait of adept sales performers. And while that's absolutely true, great sales performers also master the art of *asking themselves* better questions. The questions you ask yourself can direct your thoughts, control your mental focus, and determine how you think and feel. They can supercharge your psychology and prime your outlook to be ready for the supercharged selling state. We ask ourselves questions all day long—but do the questions make us feel better, or do they make us feel worse? Taking control of your questions can start your day off on the right foot, help you handle challenging sales calls, and pull you out of a negative state.

A coaching client of mine, Jim C., was a pharmaceutical rep who had just been assigned a completely different territory, had gotten a new boss, and had been told to learn two new drug indications, all at once. Jim had been number one in his region and had enjoyed recognition, nice commission checks, and what seemed to him like a very secure future. Jim asked me questions. "Why would the company treat me, the number-one guy, so poorly?" "Why don't they care about me?" "Why does this kind of crap always happen to me?" "Don't they realize I'll never be able to finish the year like I would have?" All these questions assumed that his sales position and his life were taking a major turn for the worse.

The negative questions Jim asked me overwhelmed his thoughts and prevented him from achieving any clear sales focus. They even overwhelmed me initially, until I remembered that we could change the questions. When I asked Jim to elaborate on just one positive thing that was happening somewhere in his life, he responded, "Well, I have a newborn baby girl, Ashley. Here, look; look at her picture!" Amazingly, Jim's state shifted before my very eyes, because he now responded to a different question than the ones he asked himself.

I started in again, "Now, Jim, in your wildest thoughts, what could be one good thing that might come from all these changes in your company?"

"Well, if I do as great a job in my new territory as I did in my old one, I'm golden," Jim responded.

"What do you mean, golden?" I asked.

"I mean that by having a new boss now, if I can blow my numbers away like I did before, I could have two regional managers pulling for me to be promoted to regional manager myself, which would be huge." Jim exclaimed.

"So, Jim," I said, "these changes give you a better opportunity to be promoted, if you can perform as well as before, right?"

"Yeah, that's right," he acknowledged.

Jim and I both realized that as Jim looked at his situation differently, he could empower himself to turn what seemed like a lemon into lemonade.

Asking better questions was Jim C.'s key. They turned a negative situation around and refocused his psychology on success. An accountability partner or sales coach is valuable in uncovering the lousy questions you're already using and developing more empowering ones. Asking yourself questions like, "How can I turn this around?" as opposed to, "Why does this always happen to me?" helps top sales performers keep going when problems do arise. Did I say problems? I meant challenges!

Questions can also frame a positive outlook for your day. Oprah Winfrey frequently suggests starting each day by asking yourself what you're grateful for to put you in a good mood, or state. Anthony Robbins proclaims the same strategy. When you're in the shower each morning, ask yourself questions about what you're grateful for, what's going great in your sales position or life, what you're excited and happy about, what you're most proud of, and any other positive questions that you can devise. Use empowering questions that direct your thoughts before any negative events try to pull you down.

Robbins also points out the value of asking yourself questions before bed. Ask yourself what you learned, what you gave, what you contributed, or whom you loved, so as to put your thoughts in the right place for peaceful sleep.

Here are some Power Boosters to help supercharge your psychology.

POWER BOOSTERS

- Improve your self-esteem by working on one aspect of your C-CORE (competence, confidence, commitment, and character) for the next 30 days.

- Discover your purpose, write it down, and carry it with you for the next 30 days.

- Identify one sales belief you possess that's limiting your results, write it down, and commit to changing it.

- Replace the above belief with an enabling sales belief, write it down, and look at it every morning for the next 30 days.

- Identify one enabling sales belief that you currently hold that has helped you be successful, write it down, and look at it every morning for the next 30 days.

- Write down your goals and commit to make them *your* reality.

- Start using minimovies before key sales calls.

- Practice saying your purpose statement and goal affirmations every morning aloud for 30 days.

- Develop a written incantation sheet for all your goals, following the guidelines.

- Develop a set of morning questions and evening questions to direct your thoughts, and practice using them for 30 days.

- Monitor your challenging situations to see if you can ask yourself better ones.

- Consider getting a sales coach to help you develop the habit of framing better questions more consistently.

SUPERCHARGE YOUR PHYSIOLOGY

The supercharged selling state, which is the fuel that runs your high-performance "sales machine," is always the result of both psychology and physiology. Everyone knows that the way you feel psychologically and emotionally affects the way you feel physically. But most people fail to recognize that the opposite is true as well. When you react or perform physically, you also are altered psychologically. When you use your body differently, you change the way you think, feel, and act. Changing your physiology by how you use or move your body even changes your biochemistry.

Michael Jordan, perhaps more than any athlete we have ever seen, had the ability to *supercharge his physiology* and *consistently* enter a peak state at will. He's ranked first in NBA history for points scored per game (31.0), he was awarded the NBA's MVP of the year five times, he holds the NBA record for most consecutive seasons leading the league in field goals (10), he holds the NBA record for most consecutive games scoring in double digits (842), and he led the Bulls to six NBA championships. The man was an awesome role model of someone who turned on his physiology to change his *state*. While he also used a psychological edge, he knew that physiology was the absolute quickest way to change his state and produce dynamic results on cue. He had an absolutely un- canny ability to turn it on and hit those shots right at the buzzer, when the pressure was on. He refused to just go with the flow and let external events direct his state.

What do you let direct *your* state? Remember, mind and body are in- separably connected. Imagine that you're driving down your favorite road in a brand new car, listening to your favorite music, having just closed the largest sale of your life, and you're on your way to pick up your sig- nificant other to depart for a Maui vacation. Would you be in a resource- ful state, perhaps a peak state? Absolutely! Now you look in the rearview mirror and discover the flashing blue lights on the police car behind you, pulling you over for speeding. Does your state change? What hap- pens to your physiology? What happens to your breathing? Is it shallow or deep? Are you looking up with shoulders confidently back or looking down with shoulders hunched forward? Do you have a big smile or a fur- rowed brow? Do you have sweaty palms? Are you nervous? How fast did your state change for the worse? In an instant! What if you could put yourself in a peak state in an instant, feeling unstoppable passion, before every sales call? Just like MJ, sales superstars do exactly that.

People all over the world have discovered that changing your physi- ology is by far the easiest, fastest, and most reliable way to change how you feel. In America, every single morning, millions of adults find an easy way to change their physiology so they feel better. What do they reach for? Coffee, of course. And at 5:00 PM, after they've experienced a fair amount of frustration and possibly some sales rejection, they want to feel better again, the easy way. What do they reach for? Alcohol, of course. Are there any "chocoholics" reading this? Why do you like that big, creamy piece of triple-fudge cake? It changes the way you *feel*. Coffee, alcohol, drugs, cigarettes, and sugar are all popular because they instantly change your physiology to make you feel better. Now, I'm not here to bash those substances, but I want to make crystal clear why you use them, if you do. Because physiological change using substances is so quick and effective, it's the most common strategy.

> *Where the body goes, the mind will follow.*
> **—GEORGE LUDWIG**

But there are many other, more empowering, ways to change your physiology and the way you move your physical body. Changes to your posture, breathing, muscle tension, and body movement, including gesturing, all work very effectively. These are techniques you can do on the spot, before and during every sales call. They are similar to the techniques that MJ used to flip his switch on and go for the dunk or three-pointer.

Exercise, meditation, music, and humor all have major effects on your physiology, too. Music and humor are particularly powerful because they affect both your physiology and psychology, and they can be employed easily throughout every selling day. Your health habits determine the energy you have available to change your physiology. Entering the supercharged selling state takes a lot of energy!

Okay, so how did Michael do it? How did he consistently change his physiology to change states, and how can we use it to increase sales? How do you use the Power of Real Passion and supercharge your physiology? First, you must have an *energy reserve* to draw from. Selling requires an enormous amount of energy, and the top pros build their reserves accordingly. Second, you must be able to simply *turn yourself on*. You need to be able to step into your peak physiology consistently and, at will, join the ranks of the selling elite.

Have an Energy Reserve

Big commission checks, Glamour Trips, sales awards . . . none of these matters if you don't have your health. You don't want to be the richest salesperson in the graveyard. Your career longevity begins with your health. Working long hours is the norm for top producers. Your body will not make the haul if you don't take care of it.

The good news is that the more you care for your health, the greater the energy reserve you have to draw from at crunch time. Chronic fatigue, insomnia, headaches, ulcers, or even heart attacks can result from an inadequate energy reserve. The bottom line is this: you've got 75 trillion cells in your body, and you must care for them to build an energy reserve and preserve longevity. (I want you to be around to buy my next book!)

Energy is a major passion of mine. I've spent a lot of time, research, and personal testing to determine what works to raise energy and what doesn't. Many clients who have hired me to inspire and teach their group have told me later that they hired me partially because they liked my incredibly high energy. Energy is contagious. People want to buy energy, so you have to bring megaenergy, like Michael Jordan did, to serving and selling your clients. Dunk it, baby!

We are not limited by our old age; we are liberated by it.
—STU MITTLEMAN

I'm going to share with you what works for me and what I've seen hundreds of other sales pros practice. I'm a sales doctor but not a medical doctor, so please get any medical advice you need before following my health suggestions. My health advice is for increasing your energy reserve, which is crucial for becoming a sales superstar. Here are my tips.

Sleep. This one is obvious. Sleep seven to nine hours per night, depending on your particular needs. Mind-body authority Deepak Chopra reminds us that restful sleep recharges and reinvigorates every system of the body. Sleep repairs worn cells and creates new ones. Sales superstars need to think creatively on their feet, and that can't happen very easily if they're not well rested.

Drink up. Drink plenty of water. Divide your weight by two to determine approximately how many ounces of water you need per day. Being even 2 percent dehydrated will radically reduce the energy reserve you have to draw from.

Aerobic exercise. Aerobic exercise is the single best technique that I have found for building an energy reserve. If there is a fountain of youth—and there isn't—this would be it. Those 75 trillion cells in your body need three basic things: oxygen, a way to eliminate toxic waste from your cells and bloodstream, and nutrition (including water). Oxygen allows the energy-producing workers of the cells, the mitochondria, to do their work. Aerobic exercise gets the heart beating faster, which increases the amount of oxygen sent to the cells. It also causes you to sweat, which clears toxins from your cells. In addition, aerobic exercise releases endorphins, which are natural stress relievers and antidepressants. Stress is a huge energy robber for salespeople, rookie or veteran. Aerobic exercise also conditions the body to draw from its reserve when needed, like an important sales call or dunking a basketball, for example. Learning to breathe properly, before and during sales calls, also increases your oxygen levels and energy. I recommend three to five days per week of aerobic exercise, even if it's just walking. Drop the remote control and get out the door!

Resistance training. Strong muscles are needed to maintain an energy reserve. Maintaining muscle will make you look better, feel better, exude more confidence, increase energy, and improve your health. If you want to move like a champion, gesture like a champion, and walk like a champion, then you must emanate the energy and power of a sales champion. After age 30, you begin to lose muscle at the rate of approximately 1 percent per year. Resistance training also maintains your bone mass, which helps prevent osteoporosis and broken bones. Research shows that people of any age can add muscle. I recommend one-and-a-half to three sessions per week, depending on your current fitness condition and goals.

Flexibility. Flexibility improves energy and power, both physically and psychologically, and gives you complete access to your energy. Develop a daily stretching plan. Try yoga or Pilates, which will increase both strength and flexibility.

Nutrition. To increase your energy reserve, you must make sure that all your cells get the nutrition they need. Follow these guidelines to raise your energy levels.

- Excess caffeine, alcohol, processed sugar, meat, and fast food all lower your energy reserve.

- The more fruit, vegetables, and fresh vegetable juice you have per day, the greater your energy reserve.
- Eating breakfast increases your energy reserve.
- Eating consistently increases your energy reserve.
- Alkalizing your diet by ingesting vegetable juices, green drinks, water, or alkaline-rich food sources increases your energy reserve. Your body strives to keep a bloodstream PH of 7.36. When excess acid enters your bloodstream from caffeine, alcohol, excess meat, or sugar, the body must waste energy to shuttle the excess acid from the bloodstream out to your cells to maintain the proper PH.
- Adding appropriate nutritional supplements or vitamins to your diet increases your energy reserve.

Establishing an energy reserve primes your physiology to step into the supercharged selling state. All you have to do is learn to throw the switch and turn on a more resourceful physiology.

Turn Yourself On

When's the best time to make a sale? Right after you just made one! Why? Because your state is totally optimized for selling. To learn how to enter a peak performance state at will, you've got to know what it feels like to be in one. Recall a time when you felt really powerful, when you were "in the zone" and firing on all cylinders. How did you stand? How did you walk? How did you breathe? What did your face feel like? Burn that image into your memory—it's the template for your peak state. Your template will be personalized and specific just to you. My supercharged state might be fast moving and rapid, while yours could be more focused and calm. The key is to remember the physiology you used when you were at your selling best.

Re-creating that state at will begins with acting *as if* you were already in it. Assume the posture and stance that's in your template. Walk in the same manner. Breathe the same, have the same confident face, and use the same voice to say your incantations. Continue practicing your state until you achieve it.

Now, this may all seem incredibly simplistic, but the bottom line is that it works. We use this principle in all our seminars when we have participants break boards. We coach them into their supercharged state of unstoppable passion and make sure they're aware of how they're standing, breathing, moving their arms, even grunting. We ask them to behave *as if* they knew they could break the board, and then they do just that! By pretending they're confident, they actually become confident. That state becomes their template to which they can always refer in the future—and they've anchored that state to the sweet taste of success and achievement.

Michael Jordan knew that to get in the most resourceful state necessary to play all-out, he had to use his physiology in a particular way to have access to all his energy and power. He had to run a particular way, move his arms a particular way, breathe a particular way, *even hang out his tongue* in a particular way to pull from his memory the exact physiology that allowed him to get switched on and take his state to the next level. You and I must do the same in selling.

> *Emotion is created by motion.*
> **—ANTHONY ROBBINS**

Remember Sally P. and her aversion to telephone prospecting? Because she was supremely confident with her clients face to face, she developed a five-minute ritual visualizing herself with them and putting her physiology in overdrive before she made her calls. She would crank her music, do a minute or two of a Tae Bo workout tape, and then say aloud her new affirmations about being great on the telephone. She e-mailed me a month later that she felt so confident after her five-minute ritual, she couldn't wait to get to the phone.

You've probably noticed that our examples have all included music, which has an incredible impact for changing states. Music evokes feelings and responses that can change your physiology instantly. Dozens of top sales producers interviewed for this book told me that they regularly put on special music before big sales presentations or in their cars as they were driving to their first call of the day. Find music that just seems to put you in the state that matches your template, and use it often. Humor can also radically change physiology and is especially useful if you're in a negative state. And, if you can laugh no matter what state you're in, you are tapping into the divine energy that loves all, heals all, and empowers all.

Here are some Power Boosters for supercharging your physiology.

POWER BOOSTERS

- Build an energy reserve with better sleep, water consumption, resistance training, and stretching habits for the next 30 days.

- Build an energy reserve by committing to implement regular aerobic exercise for the next 30 days.

- Commit and practice one or more of the energy-enhancing nutrition strategies for the next 30 days.

- *Do this right now.* For just five minutes, practice putting your physiology into *your* most resourceful selling state.

- Experiment for 30 days trying to adopt and improve your physiology for selling. Think of Jordan or some other person whom you admire and try copying them.

- Experiment with music and humor to see how they improve your physiology and state as they relate to selling.

Learning to control your physiology means that you can enter your peak performance state more consistently. When this is combined with a strong psychological foundation and ability to control your mental focus, you can sell from the supercharged selling state, leveraging it so your buyers love to say *yes!* The final section of this chapter will recap the techniques we've studied, then show how to apply them in a real-life sales example.

APPLYING THE SUPERCHARGED SELLING STATE

Professional football players have to get into peak state 16 games a year, plus playoffs. Professional basketball players must step, switched on, onto the hardwood 82 games a year, plus playoffs. But no athletes, not even professional baseball players, have to suit up as much as professional sales producers do—you've got to crank it up a minimum of

200 times per year. With so many game days, it's very easy for sales pros to slip out of their peak selling state. If you want to stay at peak levels, you'll need to get some daily *prime time.*

Get Some Prime Time

Just like a water pump that must be primed before use, your psychology and physiology must be primed every day. One hour every selling day spent supercharging your psychology and physiology will increase your sales fitness. This is time where you build your foundation by reviewing your purpose statement, adopting better sales beliefs, and investing in your C-CORE. You focus on your goals, repeat your affirmations, run your mental movies, and develop empowering self-questions.

Every day should also include time to build your energy reserve with aerobic exercise, resistance training, or stretching. Practice putting your physiology in peak state by acting *as if,* using music or whatever other techniques get you game ready. Develop a ritual of priming both your psychology and physiology that works for you. This is your daily prime time, and it's designed to send you out the door like a selling gold medalist.

Real-Life Application

In 1997, I entered a large teaching hospital in Chicago to try to get a commitment for a $700,000 purchase order of sterilization equipment. I needed to be in the supercharged selling state, and here's how I accomplished it.

Prime time. That day I got up at 6:00 AM, drank a quart of water, and had a cup of half-strength Swiss chocolate almond coffee. I read spiritual material for 15 minutes to invest in my C-CORE. I went for a 30-minute run that built my energy reserve and primed my physiology. As I ran, I listened to an inspirational tape that boosted my self-esteem and confidence, priming my psychology. Upon returning, I read a bit from a sales book and then wrote down my prayers. I asked myself some empowering questions about that day's meeting while I showered. Next I enjoyed a healthy breakfast with fruit, greens, vitamins, and more.

After breakfast, I spent about ten minutes listening to some high-energy Motown music, reading my long-term goals and purpose aloud, and reviewing my goals for the day's sales calls. I jumped into my Porsche, popped some Des'ree in the CD player, and pulled away feeling supercharged. My daily prime-time ritual left me ready to go!

Presales call. You'll also need a five-minute to ten-minute ritual to reprime yourself into a supercharged state right before you meet the buyer. Remember how the Northwestern Mutual reps spend five to ten minutes in their cars running a mental movie of serving their potential buyers and getting their commitment to purchase? Again, you need to find what ritual or technique works best for you.

When I arrived at the hospital, I stepped into the restroom and waited until everyone had exited. I then slammed the palm of my right hand martial-arts style against my right chest muscle several times, winked in the mirror, and said, "It's show time, baby! You're the best. You're the best. You're the best. They want to be served. They want to buy. This is their time. This is my dream. These are my people. I will claim you!" Popping my chest while I repeat this brief incantation always puts me in my peak state. I still use this ritual whenever I can before I make a sales visit, a big phone call, or a speaking engagement. Many people think I'm crazy, but I don't care, because it works for me.

Sales call. You need to maintain your supercharged selling state throughout the call and anchor those feelings to your product or service so that you can prompt the buyer into that state, too. It bears repeating that *buyers don't buy products or services—they buy states.* They buy the emotional state they associate with you, your product, or your service. Remember that Gary L.'s team changed their selling approach to selling *feelings* or *states,* instead of focusing on just homes. Sales superstars are state prompters. They induce a positive state and then anchor that state to what they're selling.

Why do the Gap and Nike pay Madonna and Tiger Woods, respectively, big money to sell their products? Why do politicians always like to be seen with hot dogs, apple pie, and the American flag? These people or symbols are powerful anchors in our culture. Advertisers know that if they can attach the feelings you have for these people or symbols to their products, you'll be more likely to purchase them. Advertisers have figured out a precise formula of how to prompt you into a desirable state in just 30 to 60 seconds and then anchor that state to their products. Sales pros do the same thing. They enter the sales call in such a powerful state that they pull the buyer in. They get the buyer's attention by the power of their state, then progressively shift the buyer's state during the visit. The buyer begins to pick up your energy and associate those positive feelings with what is being sold.

If you expect to prompt a positive state in the buyer, you must communicate with all of your physiology. Communication consists of factors that are both verbal (your words) and nonverbal (physiology—vocal tones and body language). You're selling with not just your choice of words but also with your tonality and body language.

From the diagram, it's obvious that top sales producers must excel in their ability to use their physiology to prompt someone into a buying state. You've probably seen people trying to sell something with their words while their body language was saying something entirely different. That is what's known as an *incongruent state,* and it must be avoided in all selling efforts. Sales pros gesture, sit, stand, and walk with energy, passion, and enthusiasm.

A mighty flame followeth a tiny spark.
—DANTE

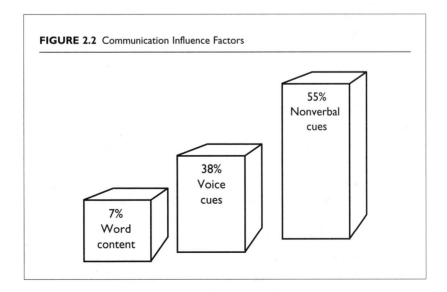

FIGURE 2.2 Communication Influence Factors

55%
Nonverbal
cues

38%
Voice
cues

7%
Word
content

To be a state prompter, you also must be able, on cue, to ratchet up your enthusiasm even higher to make things more exciting for the buyer. Remember MJ at the buzzer. You have to be able to put yourself into enthusiasm overdrive, especially if things have slipped into a lull. Transferring enthusiasm from you to the buyer must be like an electric arc. The spark—your conviction in what you're selling—transfers to the buyer and lights them up. Professional purchasing agents are visited every day by loads of salespeople who all but put them to sleep. Here's a no-brainer for you—no one will buy if they're asleep.

When you're with the buyer, your state has to be so exciting that the activity itself is wonderful. The act of showing genuine excitement in what you're selling moves people. You need to look at each sales encounter as you would a great meal. The buyer is dying to taste it. You want them so excited that they feel *yes* in every fiber of their soul. You want your sales call to be so enjoyable and stimulating, that it's absolutely the best thing they'll experience in their entire day.

The energy in the boardroom where I was making my presentation took a major dip as the hospital's clinical engineer voiced his reservations to me and the eight high-level buyers on whether to purchase this new technology or stick with the older technology around which the specs had been written. Bob was concerned about whether the new sterilizers would really work from a process standpoint in the tight quarters of their newly constructed facility across the street.

Before Bob chimed in, I had been on a major roll—in a kick-butt, take-no-prisoners kind of state—and was very close to prompting their collective state toward a yes decision. After patiently hearing him out and several other follow-up comments, I decided it was time to ratchet my state into warp overdrive.

I said enthusiastically, "Let's just take a stroll over there where I can walk you through the process, show you where everything will fit, and go over the time and money savings advantage of this process." Everyone agreed, and we filed on out. On the way, I chatted with several buyers, asking questions and replying with real enthusiasm. Their state began to improve just from the walk, which involved *their* physiology and my excited demeanor.

Once we arrived, I went right into a high-energy, five-minute presentation. I addressed all their concerns and involved several of the key buyers in standing and moving in different places as part of the presentation. The energy was continuing to build. Next, I summarized the cost savings and shared how those savings could be used to help with another important project that I had uncovered. Their faces began to light up like halogen bulbs as they looked at each other and nodded excitedly. Even Bob nodded and said, "This can probably work."

Less than 90 days later, I walked out of that same hospital with the largest single purchase order to date for that division of Johnson & Johnson. When I saw that $700,000 order come through on my fax machine, what do you think happened to my state? It went into a state of sales *ecstasy* (which is just about the most fun you can have with your clothes on!).

I trust you're sold on the power of the supercharged selling state to put more money in your pocket. Let's cover the Power Boosters you'll need to apply the Power of Real Passion to every sales day and every sales call.

POWER BOOSTERS

- Practice carving out some prime time every selling day for the next 30 days.

- Experiment and practice a five-minute or ten-minute presales call ritual to supercharge your state.

- For the next 30 days, monitor your state in very call.

- Try using your physiology more to communicate energy, passion, and enthusiasm.

- Practice dialing your state up a notch, when needed, to increase your enthusiasm.

LET'S RECAP

You don't have to be "Captain Underpants" to become a sales superstar, but you do have to unleash your real passion to increase sales results dramatically. Unleashing your passion comes down to *selling in the supercharged state.* Your sales performance this year, and in the years to come, will depend less on your ability and more on what state you consistently sell in. Remember that stepping into a supercharged selling state comes down to your taking charge of your psychology and your physiology.

Supercharging your psychology begins with building your psychological foundation, focusing on your goals, and directing that three-pound computer that's between your ears. If you're driven by a compelling purpose like Carol R., set empowering sales goals like Mark Victor Hansen does, and direct your thoughts the way that Todd B. and Jim C. did, you'll take charge of the 80 percent of what separates the rookie from the top pro. When you change your thinking, you change your life.

Supercharging your physiology begins with building your energy reserve, then turning yourself on. When you take charge of your physiology, you can hit a three-point sales quota right at the buzzer, just like MJ did.

When you commit to getting some prime time every day, supercharging your state before every call, and being an excitable, enthusiastic, dynamic state prompter with every single buyer, you might as well start shopping for a bigger home now—because it will soon be yours.

Real passion occupies a spot on the DNA of every sales superstar. Passion is a power that needs activation, though, to be unleashed. It's when you enter the supercharged selling state that you turn on the power of passion. We all have the power, but sometimes we neglect to flip the switch.

Legend has it that a woman living on the seashore of Ireland at the turn of the century was one of the first to have electricity installed in her home. It surprised her neighbors, because even though she was wealthy, she was quite frugal.

A month after installation, a meter reader knocked at her door, and he inquired if her electricity was working. She assured him it was. He then asked her why the meter showed hardly any usage. He asked her, "Are you using your power?"

"Of course I'm using it," she replied. "Every night when the sun sets, I turn on the power and lights long enough to light the candles. Then I turn the power off."

She had the power but wasn't using it. You have the Power of Real Passion, but you must turn it on to be a member of the selling elite.

3

THE POWER
OF RESEARCH

Prepare . . . or Feel the Pain

Forewarned, forearmed; to be prepared is half the victory.
—CERVANTES

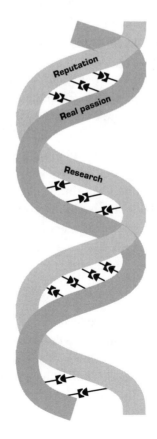

Ken S., a former sales superstar for Johnson & Johnson, tried to sell a revolutionary, environmentally friendly sterilization technology throughout his West Coast territory in 1993. He experienced a lot of resistance from hospitals in the Puget Sound area of Washington, because they were quite happy with their existing sterilization technology and suppliers. Ken knew that a little research might help him overcome their objections. He spent many hours in the library and finally discovered that an Air Quality Board, based in Seattle, was currently reviewing emission levels from existing hospital sterilizers in the area. Ken went to the board's administrator and discovered that they would soon be passing legislation that would tax, regulate, and eventually limit the emissions from all existing sterilizers used by area hospitals. He then put together a summary, with the board's blessing, and promptly visited every hospital in the Puget Sound area within 90 days, emphasizing that his product produced no toxic emissions.

The result was nothing short of spectacular. Within the year, Ken sold nine sterilization systems, worth close to $1 million in sales revenue, in the Puget Sound area alone. He became the number-one salesperson for his division that year, partially because he knew that when you prepare . . . you don't feel the pain. Ken S. was utilizing one of the most important sales strategies, the Power of Research.

If genetic researchers were deciphering a sales superstar's DNA to crack the sales code, they would uncover the Power of Research as the third molecular strand in the blueprint. Even with a *great reputation* and *real passion,* you still need to do your homework.

Just like Ken S., top sales producers in every industry gain an advantage by uncovering information that gives them a leg up on their competition. Sales superstars know that you must learn more to earn more. They work to hone their skill sets to become the very best in their company, their industry, and most importantly, in their buyers' eyes. The big sales guns know more about their buyers, their products, their competition, their marketplace, and the sales process than the rest of the pack. Their research identifies who and where their best buyers are. They consistently learn how to improve their communication skills, their self-leadership skills, and their selling skills. They study buyer psychology, time management, business, and current trends. They know that school is never out for the professional.

Sales superstars also know that their potential buyers are better informed than ever before about their needs, the marketplace, and the competition. Buyers expect salespeople to have whatever information they need immediately; if it's not provided, they'll migrate elsewhere. On the other hand, buyers can also flounder under too much information and knowledge. They don't have time to filter through all the available information as it relates to their needs and wants, and a great salesperson can provide real value by sifting, narrowing, and sorting through what's relevant to their needs. Sales superstars differentiate themselves by using research to provide a benefit tailored to the needs of a specific buyer.

In understanding how, why, when, where, and what to research, sales superstars model themselves after the most competent medical doctors. They become Doctors of Selling as they examine, diagnose, and prescribe treatment for their potential buyers. Although we most often encounter physicians in their roles as practitioners or healers, all of the advances in medical science ultimately come about as the result of solid research—it's the foundation upon which all clinical work rests. Likewise, top salespeople initiate their sales process from a solid base of research. They constantly collect relevant information and increase their knowledge to give their patients—the potential buyers—the best treatment available. In short, they become *the* specialist: they participate in ongoing *continuing education,* they *collect a complete family history,* and they *conduct a thorough assessment* in their role as a Doctor of Selling.

BECOME THE SPECIALIST

Physicians must complete an extensive educational process before they're allowed to practice medicine. After an undergraduate bachelor's degree and four years of medical school, they must also finish a residency that can last from three to six years. This residency allows them to study a specific area of medicine in greater depth—it allows them to specialize and become the expert in a more focused area than the entire field of medicine. Sales champions do exactly the same thing. They become the specialists in the niche they serve by using research skills to learn everything possible about their industry and current market conditions.

Remember from Chapter 1 that Chuck T. knew everything about Lincoln Park real estate? He knew the industry market conditions inside and out. He knew the listings and interest rates, which everyone knew, but he dug far deeper to learn about new home developments, construction activity, bank receptivity, and property tax trends—all of which elevated him to *the* specialist status. Chuck's tenacious research armed him with all the data any local buyer would ever need and built the reputation he depended on.

Cindy L., a salesperson for a major dental supply company, discovered that many of the dentists in her territory were looking for a better way to market themselves to their patients. She shared her findings with her company, and they decided to develop a cooperative marketing program based on dentists committing to a certain level of purchase volume. The program was wildly successful and came about simply because Cindy's research spotted a trend before any of her competitors did.

Get in the habit of staying on top of your industry news and trends, the opinions of experts, and competitor activity. Most of this research can be done through trade journals, business magazines, and the Internet. Subscribe to at least one trade publication for your industry, and read general business newspapers or periodicals to stay on top of your game. Get comfortable using Internet search engines to uncover industry happenings, competitor financials, and buyer initiatives. Get the fastest connection you can afford. Move as quickly as you can away from a phone dial-up to cable, DSL, or some other broadband connection. Always be looking for the latest and best Internet research tools. The information superhighway can elevate you to expert status when used properly.

Becoming the specialist also gives you an edge over the competition, because it sets you apart, enabling you to offer something to the buyer that your competitors can't. While your research includes finding out what the competition is up to, your primary focus is on the buyer and finding the *best* solution possible for their needs. You must constantly dig for new information that shows you how what you sell can be applied as a solution for their troubles. This greater differentiation makes you a specialist in problem solving with your buyers, and it positions you as the one who can help them.

Information is power.
—FRANCIS BACON

Researching your own company, its products and services, and their application to solving buyer problems and fulfilling buyer needs goes beyond knowing all the bells and whistles of what you sell. It means digging deeper to determine what strategy you must follow to position your products or services for your ideal buyer. Average salespeople learn about their company and its products and plod straight ahead. Sometimes they win; sometimes they lose. Top sales pros, on the other hand, get the newest and best information to plot a path to sales success. Sales champions relentlessly observe clients to uncover different applications for their product or service. Salespeople for a major medical instrument manufacturer discovered that a particular instrument used for orthopedic procedures was being adopted and used by cardiovascular surgeons. Discovering a different solution niche for that particular product led to a rapid increase in sales. Such research positions you as a specialist on the cutting edge who can serve new and existing buyers more effectively. Here are a few Power Boosters for continuing your development as the specialist.

POWER BOOSTERS

- Subscribe to and read at least one trade journal for your industry.

- Subscribe to and read at least one business magazine or newspaper.

- Get a high-speed Internet connection and learn to use search engines proficiently.

- Develop a constant vigilance for the solution applications for your product or service.

CONTINUING EDUCATION

Medical doctors finish a long and arduous formal education by the time their residency is over and they're established as a specialist, but their *learning* is never complete. Major advances in their fields can occur extremely rapidly, so they must constantly make time in a busy schedule to read clinical and research journals, research data on the newest drugs in the pharmaceutical pipeline, and attend seminars highlighting new technology. Lifelong continuing education keeps physicians sharp and abreast of their specialties, and it's no different for a Doctor of Selling.

> *Let us train our minds to desire what the situation demands.*
> **—SENECA**

Top sales pros are committed to continuous learning. Just like medical doctors, their education doesn't stop just because formal schooling has concluded. In fact, that's when their real schooling actually begins. *Power Selling* helps close the gap left by most college curricula on real-world selling and is part of your commitment to self-improvement and learning. Jim Rohn always said, "Your formal education will make you a living, but your self-education will make you a fortune." Congratulations for being on this journey!

We've already learned in the first two chapters that sales superstars make the time to invest in themselves. They continually improve their skill sets in psychology, finance, communication, time management, and leadership to develop greater competence, which builds confidence and a solid identity. Lifelong learning strengthens your reputation as the specialist, improves your psychological foundation, helps clarify your goals and purpose, and is a key part of the daily prime time that's vital for maintaining the supercharged selling state.

In addition, it can break through the barriers to sales stardom that fear creates. Nervous anticipation of a new potential buyer meeting, a string of phone prospecting calls, or a sales visit where the buyer will make their final decision can all be remedied by thorough preparation. Fear in sales is nothing but a wake-up call to be more prepared. Consistent education is essential to reaching your true potential in sales—or in life. In my book *Wise Moves*, I shared an acronym I developed, PANG, which stands for Perpetual And Never-ending Growth. Every sales superstar I've ever met or trained is committed to constant learning. Their commitment to the philosophy of PANG means that they've developed a hunger to grow and improve. They've got a Hunger PANG!

There are essentially two things that will make you wiser—the books you read and the people you meet.
—CHARLES "TREMENDOUS" JONES

How, where, and when you continue your education is up to you. The key is developing the habit. Learn from books. Jim Rohn always says, "Leaders are readers," and I'm here to tell you that Jim is right. I wouldn't be doing what I am today if it hadn't been for the more than 1,000 titles I've read over the course of my sales career. Experience alone won't take you to the top. Listen to audio programs or books when driving instead of only the radio. Twenty minutes a day will give you more than 100 hours per year to leverage the power of learning. Learn by reading magazines, newspapers, trade journals, and Internet sources. Learn from others and learn from your own everyday experiences, too. Personal coaching can also provide you leverage and accountability that lead to learning.

If you invest an hour per day in your education, you'll rise right to the top of the sales kingdom. It takes self-discipline, but the rewards are worth it. Learning is your springboard to a more favorable future. Here's how it paid off for Bob J.

Bob J., a real estate salesperson for Century 21, attended our sales seminar where the Power of Research was emphasized. He told me that he had been neglecting to invest any time in personal development or in improving his sales skills. Bob then commented that his sales numbers were in the toilet, and because of that fact, he had adopted a lousy attitude. In short, Bob was in some pain. I encouraged him to make the investment in himself and his sales skills, then to call me in 90 days.

I didn't hear from him until about five months later, when he called to say that he had read four books on selling, listened to two audio programs, attended one sales rally, and was getting some prime time in every morning before he arrived at his broker's office. I started to congratulate him, but he cut me off and said, "The best thing is that I've finished in the top five salespeople for two months in a row. I'm finally making some money, and my boss asked me what medication I was on. He said I seemed different. Thanks to you for helping me see that I can never stop investing in my self-education." Bob J. is well on his way to becoming a sales superstar, because he now knows that learning is a proven pain reliever.

Here are a couple of Power Boosters that will put your continuing education into overdrive.

POWER BOOSTERS

- Read at least one book per quarter on sales. (See the Bibliography.)

- Read at least one other personal development or business book per month.

- Listen to at least one audio program per quarter on sales, success, or business skills if your position requires driving.

- Identify one area where you occasionally experience fear and commit to learning whatever it takes to make you more prepared in this area. (Example: If you experience call-reluctance fear, get a book on cold calling and learn better techniques.)

- Attend at least one seminar per year on success, business, or sales skills.

COLLECT A COMPLETE FAMILY HISTORY

Before any patient ever steps into the exam room of a physician's office, that doctor has already compiled an impressive amount of research. Patients are routinely required to fill out many questionnaires regarding their family history related to both their presenting problem and other medical and lifestyle issues. Doctors review this information before they meet the patient and begin to formulate hypotheses about the identified problem and how their treatment approaches could help this particular patient—or if the patient will require a referral elsewhere. In the same way, Doctors of Selling have conducted extensive research about their potential buyers long before their initial face-to-face appointments. Top sales producers also know what kinds of buyers most need their products or services and what strategies are most likely to help potential buyers realize that the solutions to their problems lie with the salesperson. To become a sales superstar, you must *identify your ideal buyer, thoroughly research the buyer's organization,* and *identify the best account strategy* for each buyer prior to meeting.

Identify Your Ideal Buyer

Good doctors know what kinds of patients they can treat. An orthopedic surgeon won't book appointments with someone who wants a skin rash treated—that patient would have been referred elsewhere, because physicians don't want to waste precious time with patients they can't help. Doctors of Selling are no different. Top producers know that time is their most valuable resource, and they use *sales identification* to determine how and with whom they will spend it.

> *The readiness is all.*
> **—WILLIAM SHAKESPEARE**

Sales superstars use their research skills to discover their ideal buyer. If you don't identify your ideal buyer, you'll end up trying to do business with anybody. Sales pros are far more strategic in their approach. They identify their ideal buyer, *profile* them, and then can prospect them more purposefully. The bottom line is this: you can be great in all seven strategic powers practiced by the sales superstars, but if you're with the wrong prospects, you'll end up with a big fat goose egg. You must determine the best match for you, your product or service, and your company. Average salespeople spin their wheels a lot chasing after marginal opportunities, because they hate to sit still but have never really done the research to determine who their best match is. Out of every 100 sales opportunities in any given market, territory, or niche, generally 33 percent are great, 33 percent are on the fence, and 33 percent are lousy. The top sales guns eliminate the bottom third and rapidly weed through the middle third, too. They know it's a major sales sin to waste precious time with low-probability buyers.

The best way to identify your ideal buyer is to examine your current buyers and list their best characteristics. The pros look for a great match not only from a product or service standpoint but also from a personality perspective. In short, they identify both the demographics and psychographics of their ideal buyers. Demographics in sales are specific buyer populations, but they're only the tip of the iceberg. Psychographics are far more important in determining your ideal buyer profile. They are the attitudes, beliefs, and values shared by both the individual buyer and the buyer's organizational culture.

Your ideal buyer profile is a *standard* against which you measure all your buyer opportunities. Make it in a checklist format, so that you're quickly reminded of whom you should be pursuing, based on the criteria and rating system you develop. Checklists are great insurance policies for making the right decisions. The Betco Corporation, with whom I consulted, developed a checklist and rating system so that they could identify their ideal buyers and target their best opportunities. This helped their sales team narrow their list of prospects and not waste time pursuing bad business. Some sales trainers claim there is no bad business, but they fail to understand that bad business is any business that wastes your time. Here are a few sample characteristics you can use to create an Ideal Buyer Profile Checklist for rating your buyer opportunities—you must alter them to fit your specific industry. (See Appendix B for an example.)

- *Buyer's needs.* Are they in alignment with your product or service strengths?
- *Buyer access.* Do you have access to the economic buyer, other decision makers, and any relevant buying influences?
- *Buyer sales volume.* What dollar rating should you establish?
- *Buyer sales margin.* Are they generally in an acceptable profit margin range?
- *Buyer maintenance reputation.* Are they known for being a pain to deal with, or are they easy to work with?
- *Buyer is a referral.* Is your success ratio higher with referred business?
- *Buyer loyalty to competition.* Are you pursuing out of ego or because of rational business analysis?

This sampling can get you thinking about your own industry. If you're in real estate, you may want to use the listing's dollar amount or geographic location. If you're in financial services or insurance, you may want to include income level. Pharmaceutical sales reps may want to include the doctor's alma mater or the doctor's current favorite prescription choices. Defining your ideal buyer's profile and developing a checklist for easy reference means that you'll spend less and less time with marginal or dead-end business opportunities.

Your Ideal Buyer Profile Checklist makes it easy to create a Target List of your best sales opportunities. These are the potential buyers with the highest rankings from your target list, because they're most similar to the standard you set up. Concentrate your precious time on these prospects, and watch your sales numbers soar!

Research the Buyer's Organization

Once you work from your target list and plan on setting up actual contacts with those prospects, you need to gather all the information you can about your buyer's company. The Internet is your most valuable tool to collect it quickly. In addition, company literature, personal contacts, and conversing with organizational gatekeepers can help you research their organization. This research allows you to meet with potential buyers with confidence and as an expert. To really get to know an organization, you'll need to learn about their:

- History, victories, and defeats
- Mission, vision, and direction
- History in relation to their industry
- Culture
- Current business results and the historical perspective
- Executive and management profiles
- Products or services
- Competitors
- Relationship loyalty pattern with suppliers

You'll also need to know what the organization is currently utilizing as it relates to your product or service.

Identify Your Best Account Strategy

Once you've identified your ideal buyers, developed a target list, and researched vital information about potential buyers' organizations, you must also identify the strategies you'll use to manage those accounts. Initially, you must decide the best strategies for reaching those companies. This varies by industry, but could include telephone prospecting, personal marketing (mentioned in Chapter 1), networking, referral sponsorship, and maybe even cold calling face-to-face. Telephone prospecting, cold or warm, is so important in most industries that we'll cover it in more depth in Chapter 4, "The Power of Rapport."

Sales pros also identify a specific strategy for each and every buyer. Winging it is for rookies. The pros leave very little to chance. Just as medical doctors develop a treatment plan for each patient that research has demonstrated will work, top sales producers draw up a plan that's based on research they've conducted before they meet with prospects. Devising an account strategy prior to a buyer visit involves simply assembling whatever information is necessary to position you for accomplishing a particular objective or set of objectives.

Sales superstars collect this critical information in a written format prior to meeting the potential buyer. With every subsequent visit, the pros continue to update this information and add pertinent new information. They rate their positional benchmark, or where they are in relation to the probability of eventually obtaining commitment for business. This ranges from euphoria on one end of the spectrum to panic on the other end. Positional benchmarking should be done after every visit to determine how your strategy must change to improve your position. Just as the physician adjusts the treatment plan based on patient improvement, great salespeople keep fine-tuning their account strategy after every engagement with the potential buyer. Here's the information needed prior to an engagement to create an Account Strategy Plan.

- *Account profile information.* This is the data you gather, including contact information, for identifying the characteristics of the account for comparison against your standard of your ideal buyer. You are prequalifying the potential buyer to see how well they match your ideal buyer profile.
- *Buying influences.* This is identifying the decision makers, the influencers, the economic buyer, and the coach (if there is one). This means knowing who all the players are. Who has the power to say yes, and who has the power to say no? (Sometimes they're

different people.) The economic buyer in a complex sale is the one who controls the purse strings.

- *Predicted buyer response mode.* This is predicting what level of need the buyer or the buyer's organization has and how they'll respond to your product. Are they aware of their need and dissatisfied with their current setup, or are they just ignoring the problem? You are sizing up the situation beforehand, all the while recognizing that you may be operating from incorrect or missing information.

- *Sales objectives/goals.* The top producers always have a specific set of objectives for every buyer or organization, based on the information they've gathered to date. These goals must be specific, measurable, and time driven.

- *Account strategy precall tactics.* This is pulling all of the above information together and formulating exactly how you'll engage the buyer upon meeting. This is the tactical aspect of how to open the call, the key questions for diagnosis, and any suspected solution paths.

Excelling in the research of your potential buyers' "family history" is an essential part of becoming a Doctor of Selling. It allows you to spend your time wisely with prospects so you have the best chance of providing their needed solutions, it gives you much-needed data about their organization, and it provides you the foundation for developing your account strategies. Here are the Power Boosters for collecting a complete family history.

POWER BOOSTERS

- Create your Ideal Buyer Profile Checklist with identified criteria and a rating system.

- Develop your ideal buyer Account Target List.

- Commit to creating an Account Strategy Plan for each targeted account.

CONDUCT A THOROUGH ASSESSMENT

After obtaining a complete family history, a physician continues his or her research by assessing patients after meeting them. In the exam room, a medical doctor collects more information from the patients themselves by asking questions about what's troubling them, how long their condition has persisted, and what efforts have been made to treat it at home and by verifying information obtained from the family history. The astute physician knows that the problem must be clarified and a sensible diagnostic process conducted before any treatment can be prescribed. Doctors of Selling follow an identical process—they diagnose potential buyers and their organizations to uncover any needs for the salesperson's product or service. Through careful questioning, they assess buyer problems and areas of desired growth and then lead the buyer to recognize those unfulfilled needs themselves.

All sales superstars are expert diagnosticians. They serve buyers by helping them analyze the causes and consequences of their problems. By helping the buyers understand their situation, sales masters differentiate themselves from their competitors, create learning for the buyer, and build trust and credibility. To become skilled diagnosticians, sales pros follow these four principles.

1. They diagnose before they prescribe.
2. They determine the patient's pain level.
3. They understand complex selling environments.
4. They develop great questioning and listening abilities.

Diagnose Before You Prescribe

A fundamental guiding principle for diagnosing a buyer is always to remember that you must diagnose thoroughly *before* you can prescribe. Salespeople who prescribe a solution before they've diagnosed a buyer's situation commit the most common and serious sales sin of all. If a surgeon prescribes a drug, medical therapy, or other intervention without a thorough and complete diagnosis, it's malpractice. Scores of attorneys rub their hands together gleefully whenever a doctor doesn't do a thorough diagnosis, because they know they'll have an easy lawsuit. The profession of sales should be no different. *Salespeople should never prescribe before they diagnose.*

I once traveled with a salesperson for an industrial company and we waited together in a distributor's showroom. A potential buyer walked in and began to examine a piece of equipment on the showroom floor. My companion approached the buyer and found out that he was interested in the equipment. The salesperson immediately began to recite every feature on that particular piece of equipment. After ten minutes, I could see the buyer's eyes begin to glaze over. I stepped up and said, "How are you thinking about using this?" The buyer's posture changed—he was obviously relieved to talk with somebody who actually cared about his needs. Buyers want to be heard. They don't care how much you *know* until they know how much you *care.* Diagnosing before prescribing communicates that commitment to caring.

The primary reason that buyer suspicion is always so high is that *everybody* has had a salesperson recommend that they buy something without taking the time to make them feel understood. Those salespeople never asked the questions that would diagnose the real needs and wants. They were much too impatient. They had to tell you something; they had to sell you something. Ugh! It makes me mad—it gives salespeople a bad name. Salespeople are excited—and rightfully so—to share what they know is a great solution. But anytime you say to a buyer, "You need . . . ," you're prescribing. If you're talking about *your* products, *your* company, and *your* service, then *you* are prescribing what they need. The reputation problems we salespeople experience (like when others politely excuse themselves from our company at a cocktail party to refresh a drink that's only one-eighth gone) come directly from prescribing before diagnosing.

In the same way that you want doctors to take their time diagnosing your pain, potential buyers want you to take your time as well. Doctors recognize that no one medical solution is right for every patient. Yet salespeople regularly walk up and prescribe solutions, despite the fact that the buyer only fits a profile in a most superficial way. Rattling off all about your products, services, or solutions before you've established rapport or discovered the buyer's needs is what Michael Bosworth, author of *Solution Selling,* calls "premature elaboration." Diagnosing buyers face-to-face should occupy 65 to 75 percent of your time in the sales process. A thorough diagnosis serves two critical functions—allowing you to uncover the real needs and wants and involving the buyer in a research process that builds loyalty, trust, and credibility.

Determine the Patient's Pain Level

The second principle that a Doctor of Selling follows in obtaining an accurate sales diagnosis is to start with determining a patient's pain level. Just as medical doctors must ascertain where it hurts, top producers know that they must determine a buyer's need level to see if there's a match for their product or service. Great doctors are proficient in researching a patient's real level of pain. When my mother had a total hip replacement, the surgeon asked her a few questions and had her do a couple of exercises to ascertain her pain level quickly. (I promised my mother that she would be in this book, and it's not easy getting an 80-year-old woman into a book about selling!) Doctors chart pain levels on various scales, based on their knowledge and on subjective input from the patient.

Pain levels of buyers are found in the buyers' perceptions of their needs. Buyer Psychology 101 requires you to research where a buyer is in relation to what you have to offer. Where is the potential buyer *really* coming from? Great salespeople gauge the level of receptivity to what they're selling so they don't waste time selling to someone they shouldn't. You want to work hardest with the buyers who will eventually perceive that your product will solve their problem. What makes the challenge so daunting sometimes is that buyer needs change, sometimes rapidly. Buyers change their buying-need levels based on their current state, making the sales expert's need for situational acumen always high.

Buyer needs, with respect to your products or services, exist at one of four levels. Each level has its own corresponding degree of receptivity to whatever you're selling. Buyers buy when, and only when, they perceive a discrepancy between their current situation and their desired outcome. They become motivated to buy when they associate a *state of pain or trouble* with where they are now and *a state of improvement or gain* with whatever you're selling.

The four levels of buyer need are crucial research for Doctors of Selling. The four levels are the following:

1. No need
2. Dormant need
3. Visible need
4. See *your* solution

No need. This level is self-explanatory; you can't sell air conditioners in Alaska, and you can't sell heavy-duty furnaces in Fiji. This is when *you,* the salesperson, see no potential for what you sell to a particular buyer or organization.

Dormant need. This is when the need is dormant or unseen. The buyer doesn't perceive any trouble or desire for gain—they generally feel *satisfied.* Usually the salesperson sees the need, but the buyer doesn't. Problems often arise here, because the salesperson sees the need and quickly wants to prescribe the solution long before the buyer sees the need. Premature elaboration often follows, and the prospect loses interest.

Dormant needs fall into one of four categories. First, buyers can be *ignorant* of their needs—problems and growth potential just don't show up on their radar screen. Second, buyers can be *indifferent*—they're satisfied and not looking to change. Third, they can be *overconfident*—the buyer is not only satisfied but confident that whatever you're selling will not help them. Fourth, they can *rationalize*—they may have admitted a need at one time but decided that there was no workable solution.

Buyers in a dormant need level are less receptive to seeing your product as a solution for them. Average salespeople fail miserably with buyers at the dormant need level, but sales superstars often can convert the *ignorant,* the *indifferent,* and the *rationalizing* types into sales opportunities. Later in the book, you'll see how testimonials and reference stories from similar buyers help the top pros paint a picture that moves a buyer from a dormant need to a visible need. *Overconfident* buyers are the toughest conversions and should be avoided most of the time until their perceptions change.

Visible need. Buyers at this level either perceive a problem they would like to eliminate or have a desire to grow. Patients at this level either experience some pain or want to improve an aspect of their business—they're looking for a doctor to diagnose the cause and prescribe the remedy. These two scenarios are music to the ears of top sales producers, because the buyer's need is visible to them. They're motivated to find a sales specialist who can further diagnose their situation and prescribe a solution. The questions that sales superstars ask to diagnose the problem build credibility, secure additional information, and intensify the pain or desire for gain. Sales pros ask specific questions, so that the buyer's trouble or desire for growth begins to occupy a much larger place on the buyer's mental radar and increases their motivation to act. Simultaneously, the sales pro works to codevelop a solution with the buyer that includes their product or service.

Asking the right questions can help magnify their pain and then magnify your solution. Top producers keep in mind that the buyer who is motivated from a sense of pain is always more receptive to your solution, and they ask questions accordingly. We'll learn the specifics about how to do this in the section on questioning.

See *your* solution. Buyers at this level have admitted a need, confirmed *your* diagnosis of the need, seen and/or codeveloped the solution, and confirmed *your* solution is the right prescription. In short, they see *your* solution. This patient is ready for whatever therapy the doctor recommends for eliminating the pain. The buyer wants to buy. The buyer and salesperson are working together to agree on *what* will be provided, *when* it will be provided, and *how* it will be provided to deliver the agreed-upon solution—*your* solution. Sales masters know that if the buyers are genuinely at this stage, they'll participate in bringing your solution to fruition. It truly is a win-win proposition. Buyers who don't follow through may really be at a level three and haven't truly bought into your product or service as their solution.

Understand Complex Selling Environments

The third principle that Doctors of Selling follow when they assess potential buyers is to understand whatever complex relationships their selling environments present. The levels of need described above apply both to the individual buyer and to the buying organization as a whole. There are often several buying roles or influencers in any particular organization, and they may have varying perceptions of need and levels of motivation to purchase. In these complex selling situations, you must differentiate between the buyer (a human being) and the organization.

When individual buyers overcome problems or experience growth through the purchase of a product or service, they achieve what's known as a *personal win*. It's the fulfillment of a subjective goal that meets a single person's self-interest in some way. Personal wins are different for different buyers, based on their psychological framework. Personal wins are intangible—they're those *states* that your buyer wants to experience. They're the feelings that the buyer imagines that purchasing your product or service will provide them. Family feelings, a sense of security, and the pride that comes from personal growth are all examples. You must remember that, even when you're selling to an organization, you need to focus on these priceless rewards if you expect to be successful. Personal wins vary enormously, but these are some common ones.

- Gain more influence
- Gain recognition
- Increase skills
- Enjoy more family time
- Get promoted
- Contribute to the organization
- Increase job security
- Be seen as a leader
- Achieve greater status
- Increase self-esteem

When organizational buyers overcome problems or experience growth through the purchase of a product or service, they achieve what's known as a *corporate* (or *organizational) win*. A corporate win provides measurable results that benefit the organization. A corporate win is either improving one of their processes or fixing something that has gone, or may go, wrong. Corporate wins help the organization out of trouble and lead to growth. They vary somewhat, as the following examples show.

- Higher productivity
- Better performance
- Improved ROI
- Best technical solution

- Greater reliability
- Faster/easier/better process
- Increased sales
- Improved market share
- Happier customers

Remember, though, that people buy for their own needs first, so personal wins always precede corporate wins. In complex selling situations, a great diagnosis must lead toward a win-win. The company wins, and the individual buyers win. Complex selling arenas include many individual buyers in different roles, all of which your premeeting research (family history) identified. To diagnose a complex account, you must always attempt to meet with every individual with buying influence. A potential corporate win can get derailed by buyers who do not see personal wins in your product or service.

To diagnose individual buyers, whether in a complex selling environment or not, you must research the components that make up their mindset. This is the only way you can determine what's really important to them—what makes them tick—so you can position your product or service in such a way that the buyer will anticipate a personal win through purchasing it.

The Eight-Point Buyer Checklist provides eight categories of questions that show you how to position your product to provide a personal win for the buyer and a corporate win for the organization. Here's what to research.

1. *Needs.* What does the buyer and/or the organization really need?
2. *Evaluation criteria or process.* How will the buyer decide to purchase? How will they evaluate the product? What criteria will they use?
3. *Wants.* What does the buyer really want? What do they desire that may or may not be what they really need?
4. *Beliefs.* What does the buyer believe about you, your company, your product or service, and your competitors?
5. *Interests.* What are the buyer's personal interests? Hobbies, family life, favorite sports, etc.?
6. *Mentors.* To whom does the buyer look for similar buying decisions? What references will they accept?

7. *Personal successes.* What is the buyer proud of? What have they purchased before that delivered a personal win?
8. *Psychic wounds.* Does the buyer have any ill will toward your company, you, your product, your industry, or salespeople in general?

In today's market, selling environments are more complex than ever. Sales masters understand potential buyers, their organizations, and the relationships between the two. They use the Power of Research to create a great position for their products.

Develop Great Questioning and Listening Abilities

The final principle that Doctors of Selling follow in diagnosing their prospects is that they always use great questioning and listening abilities. Just as physicians know which questions to ask each patient based on the presenting symptoms, Doctors of Selling know how to ask questions in such a way that their potential buyers come to recognize both their needs and the sales solution. All of the research gathered during the assessment comes through careful questioning of, and listening to, the buyer.

Nature does not reveal its secrets. It only responds to our method of questioning.
—WERNER HEISENBERG

Questions are critical, not just for successful research but also for successful sales overall. Neil Rackham, author of *Spin Selling*, extensively researched the relationship between questioning and sales success and found a clear statistical association. The more you ask questions, the more successful the interaction is likely to be. The majority of sales opportunities are lost because of the salesperson's failure to uncover the buyer's specific needs, which is accomplished through careful questioning.

Sales superstars know *how* and *when* to ask questions—and when not to. A confident and friendly manner is needed, as well as restraint from asking questions in a forcefully leading way. Rookie salespeople often put the potential buyer in question shock, as they fire off questions like a hard-hitting news reporter. Once you seem less interested in listening to the buyer's responses and more interested in moving right into the next question, buyers begin to feel interrogated rather than heard. When that happens, the process shuts down altogether.

Great diagnostic questioning takes time. When you take the time to ask questions about what the buyer does, how they do it, with whom they do it, and how you might be able to help them do it better, you build trust and credibility.

Great questioning won't get you far without great listening, too. Most people believe that to be good in sales, you have to be a good talker. People often say, "You have the gift of gab. You should be in sales!" Nothing could be further from the truth. As many as 75 percent of top sales pros are defined as introverts on psychological tests. They would much rather listen than talk in a sales situation. Poor salespeople dominate the *talking*, but top salespeople dominate the *listening*. According to the Purchasing Managers Association of America's annual survey, the biggest single complaint of professional purchasers, year after year, is that salespeople talk too much and listen too little.

Sales superstars practice the 70/30 rule. They talk and ask questions 30 percent of the time and then listen intently to their customers 70 percent of the time. Sales expert Brian Tracy calls listening *white magic.* His research demonstrates that listening exerts an almost magical effect on human communication. It causes people to relax and open up. You remember that top salespeople know that people don't care how much you know until they know how much you care. The big sales guns know that one of the quickest ways to show that you care is by listening.

Stephen Heiman and Diane Sanchez, in their book *Conceptual Selling,* advocate a listening method known as the *golden silence,* in which you simply pause for three or four seconds at two key places in the dialogue process with the buyer—after you ask a question and after your customer responds. Introducing these two pauses into your sales call questioning process will dramatically—and immediately—improve the quality and quantity of the information you receive. The buyer now has more time to reflect and respond with solid information and will often go on and elaborate further. By pausing after the buyer responds, you also give yourself a greater chance of really understanding them.

The golden silence will seem uncomfortable at first. So much silence may give you some nerves, but the payoffs are enormous. If you practice for even a short time, the technique will soon become second nature. The golden silence strategy leverages your diagnostic questioning to get the information you need to get the sale. Did somebody say sale? I'm getting excited again!

Most simplified sales training theory distinguishes between just two types of questions: open and closed. For years, the common theory was that open-ended questions were always better for selling and that they were a big determining factor in questioning success. The common belief was also that open-ended questions should always precede closed questions. Neil Rackham's research bears out that neither premise is accurate, especially in the large or complex sale.

In thinking about what type of questions to ask and in what sequence, given the large volume of information you need to collect, it's useful to have some kind of framework or model in which to organize your approach. Neil Rackham's excellent SPIN selling model used four categories of questions to help salespeople know what and when to ask. However, we developed a different, simpler model that has been better suited to the many companies for which we've provided sales training. The questioning model used in *Power Selling* is called RPM Questioning. RPM stands for Reality, Pain-gain, and Magnification: these are the three categories of questions necessary to move a buyer through the entire diagnostic process, from a dormant to visible need and then to your solution.

Reality questions. These questions assess the situation and perceptions of the buyer. They're generally used at the start of a face-to-face engagement to gain background information that you were unable to secure during your precall identification (family history) or to confirm your precall research data. They discover what the buyer currently uses with relation to your product or service and any other relevant information about the company that you haven't already uncovered. These questions also fill in any vacancies in your Eight-Point Buyer Checklist. Although reality questions are absolutely critical, sales superstars know that if they string together too many of these too quickly, the buyer will get bored or irritated. These questions benefit the salesperson more than they do the buyer, at least on the surface.

Betco, a floor care and janitorial supply company that trained its salespeople in the RPM model, had reality questions such as, "Can you describe your current floor care maintenance program?" and, "What is the nature of your employee training program for floor care?" These questions yielded relevant facts about the reality of the buyer's situation.

Sales superstars intuitively learn how to sprinkle these questions in very subtly, without unnerving the buyer. The pros eliminate many of the fact-finding questions by doing a more thorough job of precall research and preparing an account strategy.

Pain-gain questions. These questions uncover the buyer's true need level as it relates to your product or service. Pain-gain questions may reveal that the buyer has a dormant need or a visible need, which in turn indicates the buyer's degree of receptivity. Do they have a pain (problem or trouble) or a desire for gain (growth or improvement)? This is the heart of the diagnosis. Pain-gain questions explore problems, difficulties, dissatisfactions, or areas where the organization wants to improve. Rookies either don't ask enough pain-gain questions to highlight the issues, or else they jump ahead to prescribe the solution before finishing the diagnosis or confirming its accuracy with the buyer.

These questions are intended to lead the buyer into verbalizing a dormant need or reiterating an admitted need. This last scenario is less frequent, but sales pros all have stories of when a "bluebird" fell in their lap. You must still perform a thorough diagnosis in these "slam-dunk" scenarios, so that your credibility, trust, and rapport remain high. Many easy sales have been lost when a salesperson tried to jump the gun on an obvious and admitted need.

Betco's team asked pain-gain questions like, "What's your most consistent floor care problem?" or "What training problems are you experiencing?" or "Are you satisfied with the productivity of your floor scrubbers?" These questions are very specific to your industry and account strategy. To become a member of the sales elite in your field, you must develop a list of specific questions designed to uncover those areas where your product or service can either eliminate pain or provide gain. You must help potential buyers foresee a more favorable outcome.

Magnification questions. Average salespeople eventually become proficient at asking the safe reality questions and the more daring pain-gain questions, once they have industry experience and feel more like *the* specialist. Sales pros, however, also know how to use magnification questions, especially in large and complex selling environments. These questions help the buyer see all the negative ramifications of staying with the status quo. Sales pros build up small problems and link an undesirable state to not purchasing their solution.

Magnification questions also help buyers visualize the benefits of resolving their problem or experiencing their desired growth if they purchase your product or service—they link a desirable state to purchasing your solution. In short, magnification questions magnify the buyer's problem and magnify *your* product as the solution. Ultimately they lead the buyer to the fourth level of buyer need—the buyer sees your solution.

The key to magnification questions is the sequence. Questions that magnify the problem must come *before* questions that magnify your solution. Let's look again at some examples from Betco for questions that magnify the pain. "What effect will using your older floor scrubbers have on your payroll expenses?" "What impact does your minimal training program for floor care have on the image of your new facility?" "Will overusing your old floor scrubbers increase the possibility that one or more of them will break down in the next 12 months?" All these questions lead the buyer into feeling pain or the possibility of future pain.

Now look at questions from Betco that magnify their products as the solution to eliminate the buyer's pain or to provide the buyer gain. "How much will using the Betco high-output floor scrubbers help reduce payroll expenses?" "What benefits do you foresee by having your staff better trained to take care of the floors in your new facility?" "Why is it important not to have any floor scrubbers break down during the school year's basketball season?" The key is that all these questions lead the buyer out of pain and into a desirable state regarding your solution.

A final component of all great sales diagnosis is confirmation from the buyer that the diagnosis is accurate. You must use your questions to confirm that the pain or desire for gain is truly a part of their reality. Confirming questions summarize your understanding of the buyer's reality. An example from Betco might be, "So, the main reason you've told me that you're running over budget with your floor-care labor costs is because your floor scrubbers are very small and very labor-intensive. Do I understand this correctly?" You must ask questions to confirm that they agree with the problem before you've earned the right to present the solution. They must take ownership of the diagnosis, just like a patient must accept the diagnosis from the physician.

Remember: First you diagnose, then you confirm your diagnosis, and then you can prescribe your solution.

Diagnostic expertise separates the brilliant doctor from the so-so physician. The same is true in sales. Asking questions is the cornerstone of sales diagnosis, and the RPM model guides you into asking the *right* ones—the ones that matter to the buyer. All medical doctors, upon receiving their license, take the Hippocratic Oath to act in their patient's best interest. I encourage, and playfully challenge, you to go online now, formally take our Sales Hippocratic Oath, and print out your diploma as a Doctor of Selling. Here are the Power Boosters for conducting a thorough assessment to diagnose the buyer's situation and needs.

POWER BOOSTERS

- Go online to http://www.powersellingbook.com, take the oath to become a certified Doctor of Selling, and print out your diploma.

- Watch yourself! Never prescribe before you diagnose.

- Learn and memorize the Four Levels of Buyer Need.

- Learn and use the Eight-Point Buyer Checklist.

- Always be searching for the personal wins and the corporate wins.

- Commit to improving your questioning and listening skills using this book and at least one other from the Bibliography.

- Practice the golden silence technique for 30 days.

- Develop a list of questions for each of your products following the RPM Questioning Model's categories.

- Remember always to confirm your diagnosis before you begin presenting, or "prescribing," the solution.

LET'S RECAP

I hope you are thoroughly convinced that the Power of Research gives you the edge required to become a member of the selling elite.

Ken S. enjoyed a gigantic payoff when he rolled up his sleeves to do some extra homework, and so will you.

I trust you've taken the oath to become a Doctor of Selling. If you really commit to selling like a doctor—being *the* specialist, continuing your ongoing education, collecting the family history prior to diagnosis, and doing a thorough assessment of every buyer—you will join the ranks of "board-certified" salespeople who always cure their buyers' pain.

In Michael Crichton's book, *Jurassic Park,* Dr. Carter's expert diagnostic questioning and thorough examination of the patient revealed that the patient brought to him was not trampled by a backhoe, as had been proposed, but instead mauled by a prehistoric bird.

It has taken some phenomenal research to unravel the paleo-DNA of extinct animals for genetic mapping purposes. Just like those dedicated paleontologists, I tenaciously researched sales superstars' makeup to crack the genetic sales code. Beyond a shadow of a doubt, if we study a sales superstar's DNA under a microscope, we will find *research* on the third molecular strand, right after *reputation* and *real passion.*

4

THE POWER OF RAPPORT

Influence Psychology Is Real Magic

You will derive your supreme satisfaction . . . from your ability to identify yourselves with others and to share fully in their needs and hopes.
—NORMAN COUSINS

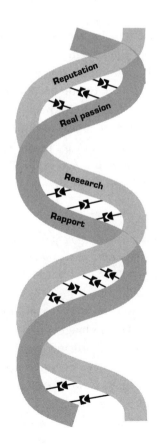

What's your definition of cruel and unusual punishment? Mine is door-to-door selling. Now I love selling and think door-to-door sales is awesome training, but the process can be very brutal to the human spirit. I first witnessed the Power of Rapport in the three months I sold Kirby vacuum cleaners door-to-door back in Indiana during a summer home from college. I would knock on the first door only to have the door slammed shut. I would knock on the second door only to be told, "Get on out of here, boy!" At the third door, I would hear, "Get the h**l out of here before I call the police!" This was no glamour job, for sure. The rejection rate was so high, I would often end the day in tears. I sold nothing day after day, week after week. After three depressing weeks of rejection, I finally got a chance to ride with Paul, a veteran of vacuum cleaner sales.

Paul had mastered rapport power—he had a magical touch as he communicated with people. He taught me how to create a great first impression. He instructed me on what to wear, how to ring the doorbell, and what distance to stand when customers opened the door. He showed me how to be unobtrusive yet friendly, how to shake their hands, and how to use their names. Paul demonstrated how to engage them with questions or humor right away, in order to get invited in. Paul averaged 12 invitations into the home out of every 20 calls. I had been invited in only twice in three weeks. Paul showed it was possible to go door-to-door with real pride.

> *If you establish common ground with your prospects,*
> *they will like you, trust you, and buy from you.*
> **—JEFFREY H. GITOMER**

But Paul's rapport power went far beyond just making a great first impression. Paul really worked his magic when he sat down with a homemaker. They always had their guard way up, but Paul slowly engaged them with a reference story or some common ground theme that established a bond. He moved his body and speech in harmony with theirs, adjusting to their particular "warm-up rate." I was always amazed by how quickly Paul got people to fall into a physical and conversational synchrony with him. His powerful and persuasive persona drew people into his own rhythm, which then allowed him to direct the interaction. He usually built a level of trust and rapport in ten minutes that most people cannot establish in the time it takes to play an entire round of golf.

That Kirby sales office applauded anyone who could sell ten or more vacuum cleaners in one month. Paul sold more than 120 vacuums in the two months I observed him. Paul outperformed everybody in that office, primarily because he had mastered the magic of rapport. As for me, I never became a sales star selling vacuums, but I did learn enough about the Power of Rapport to recognize it as the lubrication that gets the gears of the sales process turning smoothly.

The Power of Rapport establishes the levels of trust and friendship that are necessary for people to feel comfortable buying. It eliminates the buyer suspicion that lurks around every sales call. More sales decisions are made on the basis of rapport than on the technical merits of the products being sold, because people buy from people—especially people they feel comfortable with and like.

If we look under a powerful electron microscope at Paul's DNA, we would see that the fourth genetic strand is occupied by *rapport*. Even with a great *reputation, real passion,* and thorough *research,* if we don't have *rapport,* we might as well head back home.

Most sales masters use this power unconsciously, almost like a super-reflex that's part physiological and part psychological. True sales superstars can establish rapport with anybody, anytime. They can build rapport with a hospital janitor in a hallway and then stroll right over the red carpet into the CEO's office and create rapport there, too. They use rapport to put anyone and everyone at ease.

Top sales producers know that the key to building great rapport is to enter the buyer's world and make them feel understood. When you have real rapport with buyers, you can see their point of view (you don't necessarily agree with it) and communicate with them on their own wavelength. The Power of Rapport moves you from *your* paradigm of the world to the *buyer's* and back again—and makes the buyer want to come with you.

How do the masters do it? How did Paul get homeowners to warm up to him instantly? In this chapter, we'll discover what methods to pull out of the magic hat called rapport, how to use them, and how to leverage them for greater sales. In short, we'll look at how rapport is maximized through *connecting, contacting,* and *prompting.*

CONNECTING—RAPPORT'S MAGIC HAT

Sales superstars know that building rapport means connecting with buyers on as many levels as possible. Those connections form the bridges that allow salespeople to enter the buyers' world and understand their point of view. Top producers use multiple means simultaneously—their magic hat has many different rapport builders in it, because they know that one method alone does not usually create a very strong or fast connection with the buyer. Just like a dial-up modem can give you a slow, unreliable connection to the Internet, using only one means of rapport may mean that you'll get disconnected from the sale. True sales champions opt for the superfast T1 line to establish unshakable rapport rapidly. They know that they can create that magical connection with their prospects on an infinite number of levels. Their best rapport builders include *caring, commonalities, communication flexibility, likeability,* and *humor.*

Caring

The first method to establish rapport with potential buyers is simply to care genuinely about them. Disney World knows that the number-one way to create its special brand of magic for vacationers is to stock its parks with caring, attentive staff. Paul was able to befriend potential buyers right away, because he was sincere and really cared about easing their daily burdens.

Caring means that you adhere to a win-win philosophy, which underlies everything you'll learn in *Power Selling.* Win-win, popularized by Stephen Covey's book *The 7 Habits of Highly Effective People,* means that the salesperson and the buyer come out of every communication with both of their respective interests served. Win-win recognizes that buyers and salespeople need each other—a successful sale will meet *both* their needs, not just the seller's. From these mutually satisfying interactions, you may develop a genuine friendship with your buyer. Research estimates that more than 45 percent of all sales are accounted for by some level of friendship. While you'll learn more about this in Chapter 7, "The Power of Relationships," it's important to understand that caring is the seed of such friendships.

If you would win a man to your cause, first convince him
that you are his sincere friend.
—ABRAHAM LINCOLN

Caring also means that you can be honest about your motives. You don't have to hide the fact that one of the needs that gets met through a sale is that you're getting paid for it. Those bonus checks and Glamour Trips are part of what motivates you to serve your buyers well and tend to their needs. Top salespeople care for their own needs as well as those of their buyers, knowing that mutual wins keep everybody coming back for more.

Commonalities

The second means of rapport building that top sellers pull out of their magic hat is finding things in common with the buyer. Rapport begins with similarities, not differences. In neurolinguistic programming, that's known as *matching*. You can match interests by discovering similar activities or experiences. You can also match associations—by finding mutual friends, business contacts, or groups to which you both belong. Sales professionals look for every clue that will identify any person, experience, background factor, or activity they might have in common with the buyer that could help them build a common bridge.

I half-dreaded meeting Barry S., who was a very high-level hospital administrator. No one in my company had been able to establish rapport with him or close a sale, and several of our best people had tried. Fortunately, my reality questions (from the interests category on the Eight-Point Buyer Checklist) revealed that Barry was a huge boating fan and lived on the same waterway west of Chicago that I did. Barry lit up when we talked about boating and began to see me as someone who really understood his world. Long story short: This "difficult" account became easy pickings for a $100,000 order. Our mutual love of the water sparked a rapport that led to a long-lasting and mutually satisfactory business relationship.

Sales superstars also find common ground with their buyers through body language and voice tonality. Remember from Chapter 2 that nonverbal factors (posture, gestures, eye contact) determine 55 percent of any communicative message's effect, and voice factors determine 38 percent. The content of the words themselves, which salespeople typically use to build commonality, makes up only 7 percent of a message's impact. If you try to establish rapport by using only words, you're missing one of the largest bridges with which to enter the buyer's world.

Have you ever found yourself enjoying a conversation with somebody and then noticed that both of your bodies have adopted the same posture? When people have close rapport, they tend to match each other in posture, gesture, and eye contact. It's almost like a dance, where partners respond and mirror each other. Malcolm Gladwell, author of *The Tipping Point,* cites several research studies that reveal that complementary body language and conversational rhythm create a strong sense of commonality. Studies even show that babies synchronize their heads, elbows, shoulders, hips, and foot movements to the speech patterns of adults with whom they're intimately involved. It's just the magic of how we're hardwired. By matching and mirroring the body language, vocal tonality, eye contact, and rhythm of your buyers, you can quickly gain rapport with just about anyone.

> *What you can become, you already are.*
> **—FRIEDRICH HEBBEL**

Denny O., a senior sales rep and superstar in medical sales, made a sales call on Ed, a surgery director at a Rockford, Illinois, hospital. Ed had always been caustic and unresponsive to the numerous attempts by our sales personnel to get him to evaluate our intraoperative blood-recovery system. The other reps described him as closed up, both physically (arms crossed, stiff posture, and withdrawn) and conversationally (providing only yes/no responses and withholding information). The forecast was bleak for moving the sales process forward. Denny O., with me tagging along, was called in as a last resort to salvage the evaluation of our product, the Cell Saver®.

Like Paul, Denny O. had an exceptional ability to establish rapport when others couldn't. Ed was indeed closed up—his legs and arms were crossed, and he set himself at a 90-degree angle to Denny. Denny matched his body language—sensitively and respectfully, but match it he did. His weight distribution and body posture were aligned with Ed's without being too obvious. Denny moved his hands in small ways that seemed to synchronize how Ed moved his arms. He also began to match Ed's speaking pattern and rate, even though this was radically different from his natural one. Although it was obvious that Ed was determined to be difficult, their conversation began to seem harmonious. Denny also matched a couple of specific phrases that Ed used when he described his needs regarding blood recovery.

Ed shifted his body in and his elbows forward on the desk to make a couple points, this time looking directly at Denny. Denny paused, matching Ed's speaking tempo, gently brushed the desk with his elbows, and then summarized Ed's points much as he had said them. What happened next caught me totally off guard. Ed actually smiled. Denny smiled back, and then I smiled, too. (I felt like a well-trained sheep.) What I observed was that Ed was being seduced and that it was Denny who directed and orchestrated their interaction. Denny first synchronized himself closely with Ed to establish rapport, and then because he had the rapport, Denny could *lead* Ed toward the outcome he wanted. Denny's rapport-building skills, particularly his use of matching body language and voice, were so strong that Ed couldn't resist—even though he was on guard against it. Big sales guns like Denny always use matching, even though they may not be aware of it.

It's important to emphasize that matching body language, voice patterns, and vocal tonality to establish commonality is not childlike mimicry, which is usually noticeable, exaggerated, indiscriminate, and considered offensive. Matching is a natural, subtle process that you already do unconsciously. Many salespeople ask me after sales training if I consider matching to be at all manipulative. I always emphatically say no, because matching is simply a rapport-building tool that allows you to more effectively enter *the buyer's world*—and that's the best place to experience the empathy necessary to serve the buyer well.

Although it's way beyond the scope of this chapter to detail every specific step for effectively matching buyers' language content, posture, gestures, breathing, voice tonality, vocal patterns, eye contact, and more, I can offer one guaranteed key to success: *practice!* Be a keen observer of others' communication behaviors and then begin very subtly to mirror them. Pick one or two components and work on them until they become automatic. Have fun with it. Practice matching body language with family members and friends to see if you can create greater rapport in a particular setting. If you both feel closer, it's usually a good indicator that what you're doing is working. Some matching will come to you naturally, and some factors you'll have to work on. Remember this, though: any improvement you can make in quickly establishing rapport without words will pay off handsomely.

Communication Flexibility

A third connecting strategy in the magic hat called rapport is communication flexibility. Top sales masters know that they must alter their communication style to fit the characteristics of their potential buyers. The personality style, job status, region of the country, and cultural or ethnic background of the buyer all have an impact on how you need to communicate. Trying to establish rapport with an accountant is dramatically different from trying to establish rapport with a VP of sales. If you're in the Midwest or deep South, you'll need to take more time to establish rapport than if you're on either coast. The buyer usually wants to talk about where you both grew up, where you went to school, whether you have kids, and any relevant sporting news. If you skip this kind of rapport talk, buyers will be suspicious of whether they really have enough in common with you to do business. Part of Paul's magic in the Midwest was his ability to engage homemakers by talking about local school events, neighborhood gossip, and any small talk. On the other hand, if you're in New York City or Philadelphia, there is virtually no "official" rapport time. The buyer wants to get right down to business and may simply begin your visit with a question like, "What have you got to talk to me about today?" Rapport must then be built during the business of the call—matching body language and speech patterns helps until you uncover some common interests or associations.

It would be nice to have a city-by-city checklist of how to connect and establish rapport, or a guide for every personality type and job level, but these don't exist. Sales superstars remain flexible. They adapt their conversational style, voice tone, word choice, gestures, and personal space to be compatible with the potential buyer with whom they're interacting. You must be a keen observer—of your surroundings, the region, the organization, and the buyer. Use your eyes and ears and be willing to experiment with varying your approach. Top producers become chameleons of approach.

Likeability

Likeability is the rabbit in our magic hat for connecting to people and establishing rapport. If potential buyers and clients like you, they'll forgive almost anything you do wrong and still buy from you. If they don't like you, you might as well pack your bags, because even if you can memorize this book and hit every principle right on target, they still won't buy. There are several traits of the "like factor" that popular and endearing people (including sales superstars) tend to share.

> *I will speak ill of no one, and speak all the good I know of everybody.*
> **—ANDREW JACKSON**

Likeable sales pros are selfless and *focused on serving.* They are optimistic and share their convictions that everything will turn out well for the buyer. They have a sense of humility that prevents arrogance or self-absorption. They are even-tempered and never display angry or rude behavior in a buyer's presence. They have a sense of humor that keeps them laughing at themselves, and they have a personal charisma that shows they are completely comfortable with themselves.

Unfortunately, there is no cut-and-dried method to help abrasive salespeople suddenly become more likeable. However, by focusing on the traits described above and working to build them into the C-CORE of your identity, you can easily influence how buyers respond to you. When they quickly like you, rapport is easy.

Humor

Humor is the grand finale, the flourish of flowers that sales masters pull from their magic hat. Nothing builds rapport faster than humor. It relaxes prospects enough to drop their normal buyer suspicion. It can enable them to cope better with whatever stress they may be facing from a stumbling economy or corporate layoffs. Even just a minute or two of laughter from you can help. Research has demonstrated that laughter actually produces a series of physiological reactions (such as altered endocrine levels) that promote well-being and health. Humor and laughter also improve your buyers' (and your) state, making them much more receptive to establishing rapport. You don't need to be a comedian; you just need to see the lighter side of situations, particularly when you can poke fun at yourself. Are you ready for some sales humor now?

A hunter went duck hunting in Canada. At the start of the day, his tour guide issued him a hunting dog, a black Labrador Retriever named "Salesman." When he arrived back late in the afternoon, the tour guide asked how things went.

"The best I've ever seen! Salesman helped me bring in twice as many ducks as anybody else," the hunter bragged.

"Well, he's a damn good dog," replied the tour guide.

A year later, the hunter returned to Canada to duck hunt, so he requested Salesman again, which the tour guide gladly provided him. The hunter achieved the same spectacular results and again declared that Salesman was by far the best dog he'd seen in more than 20 years of duck hunting.

Two years later, the very same hunter was back in Canada, and he again found the same tour guide and requested Salesman. The tour guide replied that unfortunately, Salesman was already out working, but that he had a new dog, also a Labrador, that might work well for him. This dog was named "Sales Manager." The hunter agreed, took the dog, and left for the day.

When he arrived back in the twilight of the day, the tour guide asked how things went. The hunter replied that it had been the worst hunting day of his entire life. "Sales Manager didn't do a damn thing but sit there and bark, bark, bark all day long!"

Feel free to share this joke, especially with your manager!

Sales superstars have a magic hat full of rapport builders that they use to connect with potential buyers. They relate to their buyers through as many means as possible, so that they can easily enter the buyers' world and create a strong sense of understanding. Their magical touch with customers builds rapport quickly and firmly. Here are Power Boosters to help stock your magic hat.

POWER BOOSTERS

- Don't forget that caring is the key to connecting.

- Find common interests or associations that you have with the buyer.

- Become a keen observer, and start observing speech patterns, posture, gestures, eye contact, and voice cues.

- Practice matching nonverbal and voice patterns with friends and family to discover your additional rapport-building power.

- Be aware of regional and cultural differences for connecting.

- Practice varying your communication style (verbal and nonverbal) to match the buyer's personality.

- Make sure that you practice all the traits that make you likeable—selflessness, optimism, humility, even-temperedness, charisma, and humor.

- Have fun. Look for the laugh. Lighten up!

CONTACTING—FOLLOW THE RULES OF ENGAGEMENT

The Power of Rapport is all about building bridges into buyers' experience. We've seen that sales superstars create that magical sense of connection through as many methods as possible—they know that the more bridges they can pull out of their magic hat, the stronger their rapport with buyers will be. However, top pros also know *how* to move across those bridges—how to make contact with prospects so that they can use those methods we've already discussed. Having a hat full of rapport builders won't do much good if you don't know how to use them.

Surprisingly, you set the stage for great rapport with your buyer in just the *first 30 seconds* (or less) of contact. Because that realization can create intense pressure (you only get one chance to make a good first impression), sales masters are extremely disciplined in their initial approach with clients. Just as the rigors and anxiety of combat require mental and physical discipline of soldiers, the stress of a first encounter with a potential buyer means that you must have already established a set of procedures to guide that contact. Soldiers have learned Rules of Engagement to help them with split-second decisions when they make contact with the enemy, and you must learn the rules of successful sales engagement to establish rapport under stress.

Contacting a potential buyer occurs in one of three ways. Marketing communication pieces, such as sales letters, direct mail, and e-mail, have already been covered in Chapter 1. Face-to-face contact, which comprises over 90 percent of all selling, is the second method; telephone contact with a buyer is the third. Major sales opportunities are lost every day because the buyer concludes in the first 30 seconds (20 on the telephone) that the salesperson is not someone with whom they would like to do business. The rules of engagement described below for face-to-face contact or telephone contact ensure that those crucial seconds are used to build rapport quickly.

Face-to-Face Engagement

Although much sales literature is devoted to discussing the keys to closing a sale, very little is devoted to *opening*. Opening a sales call means making contact and engaging the buyer to set the stage for rapport and a continuing sales process. The sales "halo effect" guarantees that if buyers' first impressions of you are positive, they'll think you're better than you are; conversely, if their first impression is negative, they'll think you're not as good as you are. The following sales rules of engagement will enable you to establish rapport quickly and build a nice halo.

You must be in your supercharged selling state. To ensure that your buyer will be receptive, you must exude the confidence, enthusiasm, energy, and real passion described in Chapter 2. Research shows that buyers make an unconscious assessment about you within the first *seven seconds,* based primarily on your physiology and appearance. You must also become a keen observer of your impact on the buyer—how you present yourself can affect the buyer's breathing, heart rate, skin temperature, sweat glands, blood pressure, and even eye blinks. Make sure that your state is optimal and that your impact on the buyer is positive.

Have the appropriate image or appearance. No matter how fancy your brochure or Palm Pilot is, if your appearance is inappropriate for the buyer, you will never be able to engage effectively. If your clothes, hair, or teeth are not well-kept, you have a barrier to rapport. Your briefcase, pen, and other accessories should also look professional.

Establish equal power. When you meet buyers for the first time, you must look them directly in the eye, extend your hand first, and say your first and last name. Nine times out of ten, potential buyers will also respond with their first and last names. Now you're on a first name basis with the buyer. Double-dipping your name, James Bond style, also helps the potential buyer remember it. However, you must double-dip your first name instead of your last name. "George, George Ludwig, nice to meet you," is all it takes. Being on a first-name basis puts you on equal footing with buyers as you begin the engagement, which is very valuable in building strong rapport.

Use a standard opening line, followed by a long silence. Say something like, "I appreciate this opportunity to get together with you," and then shut up for four seconds. That pause may seem excruciatingly long, but it allows the buyer to take you in, and it communicates that you are powerful and comfortable.

Synchronize yourself to the buyer's warm-up rate. This simply means that after the silence, if the buyer wants to talk baseball, then by all means talk baseball. If the buyer wants to start talking immediately about business, then follow suit and talk about business. In short, match their "warm-up rate" with your responses.

Create a 15-second to 30-second infomercial about what general benefits you and your company provide. Also, have prepared a series of diagnostic questions you can jump right into as needed. (See Chapter 3 for a description of those questions.)

When I meet potential buyers with the intent of diagnosing whether my company can help them improve their sales practices, here's what

I say after we've exchanged names, paused for four seconds, and sat down. "We work with business leaders who want to improve their company's sales performance." The purpose of an infomercial is simply to get the buyer curious enough to inquire about whatever solution your product or service provides. You should also use your infomercial at any networking functions, trade shows, or places where you might rub elbows with potential buyers.

Telephone Engagement

Alexander Graham Bell's invention may be the greatest tool salespeople have ever known. In all but a few industries, the telephone is the primary method to set up appointments with qualified prospects. Contacting them must create the curiosity and rapport needed to proceed, because if you can't establish initial rapport on the phone, guess what? No appointment! And in sales, nothing can happen unless you get that first appointment. Telephone work ultimately drives the whole sales process by being the most cost-effective way to prospect, set appointments, begin rapport, and follow up with clients.

Given all these great advantages, you might think that phone contact is the favorite activity of all salespeople. Nothing could be further from the truth—it's the least popular and most procrastinated task. Why? Because most salespeople have had such miserable results—success ratios are as low as 3 to 5 percent—and because they fail to understand some fundamental truths about telephone contacting. They don't realize that every rejection (and there are a lot in phone work) puts money in their pockets—because getting more rejections means that you've made more calls, which means that you'll ultimately get more sales. In addition, they don't comprehend that business-to-business buyers do *not* hate to get cold calls. What buyers *do* hate is getting rude or unprofessional cold calls.

Telephone contacting doesn't need to be a millstone around your neck. You can raise your success ratio of securing appointments to as high as 50 percent, enhance the rapport-building process, and make more money by following the rules of engagement. (If money isn't important to you, please send me what you have!)

Get your buyers to call *you*. The more effectively you've built your reputation and the more personal marketing you've done, the more buyers will call you. These "warm" calls are fun! They're from potential buyers who are interested in your service or product. Such calls stack the deck in your favor to establish rapport and increase your conversion rate of calls to sales.

Call mostly *ideal buyers* from your *account target list,* not just any Tom, Dick, or Harry. Calling prequalified prospects, or warm contacts, improves your chances to establish rapport and achieve success immeasurably. This includes the warm calls where you've secured a referral from a satisfied client or have been given a sponsorship directly from one executive to another. In complex selling arenas, you must call those in power, including the economic buyer. You should call at as high a level as you can within the organization that you've defined as your ideal buyer. Be prepared to diagnose and relate to the high-level issues to develop greater rapport. You may need to call at lower levels as well, but being connected at a high level allows you better access to all the information you need to move the sales process forward toward commitment.

Be in the supercharged selling state whenever you're making telephone calls. Sound familiar? Remember—repetition is the mother of learning. Developing a precall ritual like Sally P. did can be very effective. Smile when you dial. Many top selling pros keep a mirror on their desk to check that they're smiling and in a passionate state.

Another tip for enhancing your state for the telephone is to stand up. You will sound more animated and confident and will improve the use of your diaphragm for better vocal variety and less strain on the vocal cords. Using a high-quality, hands-free headset can improve your telephone calling results significantly.

Another key to keeping in a supercharged state is to schedule brief telephone prospecting regularly. Sometimes, shorter sessions allow you to maintain your happy, passionate state, despite the inevitable rejection.

Always be scrupulously polite. Always err on the side of being polite, but never apologize for calling. That can be a rapport killer, because it takes away your equal power positioning. If the prospect, for whatever reason, is not inclined to continue conversing with you, then politely disengage from the call.

Have a purpose for every single call and get right to the point. You have to aim for something on every call. Too many salespeople pick up the phone aiming at nothing, and as my friend Les Brown always says, "They end up hitting nothing dead on the head!" You must also never dawdle on the call, but get right to the point. If you're unclear as to your specific purpose or beat around the bush getting there, rapport will break down in the first 20 seconds.

Follow a proven telephone script and make sure it includes the steps of a successful telephone engagement. Most salespeople cringe at the mention of a script, but it provides a structure to deal with the anxiety and pressure of trying to build rapport in just a few seconds.

Think of the last good movie you saw. Did it seem as though all the actors were reading from a script? Of course not—they don't sound like they're reading scripts, because they've practiced their lines until they sound natural. That's what the sales superstars do, too. If you're prospecting by phone to set appointments and realize that the success of the entire sales process hinges on the quality and quantity of the buyers in your pipeline, do you think that this is the place to wing it? No way! Many top pros use scripts so often that they virtually memorize the formula and don't have to work from a written script all the time. However, most sales veterans still review their script from time to time as a refresher or when something changes in their offering.

The first key to following a script on a cold call is to recognize that you only have a 20-second to 30-second window of opportunity. Think about the solicitation calls you get at home. When you, as the potential buyer, receive a cold call, there's a certain amount of anxiety created from not knowing the caller and not knowing what they want or expect. Most salespeople aggravate that situation by increasing the tension—by not getting to the point or by sounding tentative or uncomfortable—which reduces the interest. From the moment the buyer picks up the phone, you have 20 seconds to reduce their tension and create interest. Your number-one objective is to create enough curiosity so that rapport-building can begin to erode the anxiety of the call.

Here are the four steps of all successful telephone scripts.

1. Break the buyer's preoccupation. You need to get the buyer's attention right out of the gate, but most rookie salespeople open with some gimmicky line. This doesn't work, because people respond in kind. I was at home recently, and a financial services salesperson called to ask if I wanted to protect my family's future—a stupid question. Why? Two reasons. First, the question is so obvious, it feels smarmy and manipulative, which kills credibility fast. Second, it showed me that the salesperson had not read Chapter 3 of *Power Selling* about the importance of research, because if they had, they would have discovered that I'm single.

When you ask stupid questions, you'll either kill rapport or you'll get a stupid answer. If you ask a reasonable question or make a reasonable statement, you'll get a reasonable response. Nothing fancy is needed, because people will respond in kind. Use a polite, reasonable opening and they'll usually respond in the same way.

The very best way to break somebody's preoccupation is to open with the sweet sound of their own name *pronounced correctly.* Start by simply calling up and saying, "Good morning, Mr. Gold." That's it. Nothing fancy. Why? It works. People love the sound of their own name, and when you use it politely in a greeting, you've broken their preoccupation and have their attention. Step one is completed.

2. Introduce yourself. Simply say who you are and who your company is. If they're not likely to recognize your company, you can also insert a brief infomercial about what you do. "Good morning, Mr. Gold. This is George Ludwig with GLU Consulting. We work with business leaders who want to improve their company's sales performance." If you're calling on a specific market niche where you're *the* specialist, then you can tailor your introduction accordingly. For example, you could say, "Good morning, Mr. Gold. This is George Ludwig with GLU Consulting, and we've helped health care companies like Johnson & Johnson improve their sales performance."

Too many rookies delay revealing who they are, raising the buyer's anxiety to the point where rapport cannot be recovered. Just get your introduction in. Step two is completed.

3. Generate curiosity. The next step is to create curiosity by picking either a known buyer need (dormant or openly admitted) or a likely need that your precontact research predicted for that target buyer. You generate curiosity by mentioning a common problem or need (pain) that other clients have or a growth area (gain) you suspect would be of interest. Sales masters often create enough curiosity by painting the picture about another client's situation that the buyer begins to edge from a dormant need toward a visible and admitted need.

Remember from Chapter 3 that buyers will do more to get out of trouble than they'll do for growth, but if the pain you mentioned doesn't apply, it makes rapport building far more challenging. You can always attempt a second area of suspected pain, but if this misses the mark, too, the buyer begins to get anxious with so much fishing going on.

Let's look at an example.

> Good morning, Mr. Gold. This is George Ludwig from GLU Consulting, and we've developed customized sales processes for midsized companies like the Betco Corporation. One of the major concerns we're hearing from other VPs of Sales is that they don't have a system in place to prevent their sales team from spending too much time on the wrong activities or with the wrong buyers. We've been able to help companies like Betco deal with this issue, and I'd like an opportunity to share with you how.

This example showcases a common problem many sales VPs from midsized companies experience. Keep experimenting with your script until you have several common problems that target your ideal buyers. Develop several scripts and keep testing them until you have a couple that work.

Your desired outcome at this point in the telephone contact is simply to get the buyer to say, "Tell me more about that." If this occurs, then your 20-second opening worked, curiosity was piqued, and rapport began. The sole goal of all telephone prospecting is to get the potential buyer to say, "Tell me more," or, "How do you do that?"

The above example capitalized on a common problem facing many of my buyers. The other telephone scripting tactic is to focus on the desire for growth as a solution to a problem. The key is to experiment and determine what works best for most of your ideal buyers, your personality, and your product or service. Here's an example of a script that's designed to spark curiosity for growth.

Good afternoon, Mr. Gold. This is George Ludwig with GLU Consulting. We work with business leaders from companies like Johnson & Johnson who want to improve their company's sales performance. We've developed the finest customizable sales process and training available today, which will dramatically improve the productivity of your team. I'd like the opportunity to share with you how we do that.

Again, the goal is to simply generate curiosity about how you helped someone else. All telephone prospecting and engagement boils down to getting the buyer emotionally connected to solving a problem or experiencing some new growth, which starts building rapport with you. Step three is completed.

4. Ask for the appointment. Just as you must never prescribe before you diagnose, you must also never try to set up an appointment until you have buyer curiosity and they say they want to know more. Then simply suggest a very specific time to meet. Be so specific that it becomes a question of *when* to get together, not *whether* to get together. Here's an example: "That's great, Mr. Gold, we definitely should meet. How is next Friday midafternoon for you?" Be very specific and direct—you are a busy professional. If the time is not good, they will let you know, and they'll usually suggest a specific alternate time. Buyers respond in kind, so the more specific you are in asking for the appointment, the more specific they'll be in setting it up with you.

Develop your own telephone engagement scripts around this four-step formula and watch your rapport with buyers grow.

Always leave voice mail messages derived from your telephone scripts. If you get thrown into voice mail, be prepared to leave a provocative, 60-second (or less) message. Experiment with different voice mail messages, even trying humor, until you find a couple that lead to returned calls. Never leave the same message twice in a row for a prospect, and never leave more than a single voice mail per week, unless the prospect has returned your call.

After you've made four attempts, spread over a month, with no response, try one or two wacky, humorous voice mails before you retire that prospect for the time being. I once got a call back from a high-level sales executive after I left him a message saying that he was harder to reach than then-President Bill Clinton. He called back, and we chuckled about it—then set up an appointment.

Track all your calls. Use some type of recordkeeping system for tracking the number of calls, callbacks, leads, appointments, and meetings, as well as the prospects who have made it into your pipeline. ACT!, GoldMine, and Microsoft Outlook are popular contact-management systems that work effectively. Manual tracking, while antiquated and cumbersome, still works, too. The key is to have some recordkeeping system in place.

Tracking *all* of their sales efforts, whether face-to-face or by telephone, is something the selling elite always do. They discover what works and use that more, and they jettison those sales techniques that have led to dead ends.

By following Rules of Engagement, soldiers know what to do immediately when they encounter an enemy on the battlefield. Likewise, following the rules of engagement for contacting prospects will successfully guide you to establish rapport and make your buyers feel you understand their experience. Here are your Power Boosters for contacting your buyers to establish rapport.

POWER BOOSTERS

- Be in the supercharged selling state for telephone or face-to-face engagement.

- Review your research before engagement.

- Establish equal power by always extending your hand first. Be prepared to endure a silence as the buyer takes you in.

- Develop your 15-second to 30-second infomercial about what you and your company do.

- Make your cold telephone contact calls on ideal buyers from your account target list.

- Be scrupulously polite.

- Develop several telephone scripts based on the four-step formula. Practice until you've internalized them and you've found one or more that work.

- Remember your number-one objective in all telephone engagements is to create curiosity so that rapport can begin.

- Develop a couple of working voice mail scripts based on your telephone scripts. If you're not getting callbacks, don't hesitate getting a little wacky or humorous—what have you got to lose?

- Track all of your calls as well as all your sales activities to improve efficiency and effectiveness.

PROMPTING—INDUCING THE MAGIC

If you've ever played with a kitten, you know that it will follow your hand motions. If you wave a piece of string to the left, it jumps to the left. If you move the string to the right, it follows to the right. As long as you keep the kitten captivated, you can prompt it to move in any direction you want. Likewise, if you establish strong enough rapport, you'll be able to prompt buyers to follow your lead, too. That's the magic!

Understanding how rapport is established with a buyer can be very useful. As you become a keen observer of the connections and commonalities that you and the buyer have established—including shared interests, associations, common phrases, verbal patterns, and nonverbal factors—you'll increase the likelihood that you can lead the buyer toward a commitment to purchase. Remember from Chapter 2 that people buy *states*—the feelings they associate with you, your product, or your service. Top sales producers establish strong rapport to induce a positive state in the buyer and a willingness to purchase. In short, they become *state prompters*.

In the real-life application in Chapter 2, you saw how valuable the supercharged state is when selling. Now you want to bring the buyer into that state as well. To prompt that emotional buying state in the buyer, you first must test your level of rapport to make sure it's strong enough before leading the buyer forward. That's accomplished both verbally and nonverbally. You must monitor and match verbal clues such as volume, tempo, tonality, and vocabulary choices and adjust your behavior accordingly. Savvy buyers often don't want to reveal how much rapport you've established with them. Because of that, nonverbal cues may serve as the fastest, best predictor of your ability to lead the buyer.

I sat in on a sales call between a new pharmaceutical salesperson, Mitsy K., and a doctor. In the middle of the 25-minute meeting, both the doctor and Mitsy were sitting all the way back in their chairs. A few minutes later, Mitsy suddenly leaned forward and started talking about all the patients that had been served by a particular drug. Within about three minutes, the doctor leaned forward, too. I could feel the trust build as they conversed back and forth and knew they'd hit it off. Closing the sale and getting commitment seemed like a piece of cake at that point.

Whether consciously or not, Mitsy had leaned forward because she sensed it was the right time. Rapport was strong enough that Mitsy knew it was time to test whether she could lead the doctor. Mitsy knew that if the doctor leaned forward, too, she was enthusiastic about the new drug. She also knew that the doctor would be giving a nonverbal clue that she was adopting Mitsy's state—a state of real passion about what Mitsy proposed. You have to love the magic of influence psychology.

In Chapter 2, I led a group of hospital decision makers for a stroll to another facility to kick up their state a notch. If they had declined my offer, it would have been obvious that I needed to work further on rapport or research their needs more carefully. When you lead buyers nonverbally and they follow your lead, you prompt their state toward commitment, whether you're conscious of it or not. Additionally, whenever you get buyers involved physically, their emotional investment increases. Getting them to walk with you, handle your brochure or product, drive the demo car, walk the property, or push the equipment's button all increase their emotional connection to you and your product.

In summary, you lead buyers verbally and nonverbally to prompt a buying state. The more they follow you, the stronger your rapport, and the greater their readiness to purchase from you. Here are Power Boosters for prompting your buyers to purchase.

POWER BOOSTERS

- Be in a supercharged selling state.

- Monitor their state, particularly their nonverbal factors.

- Try leading them nonverbally and monitor whether they follow your lead. If not, go back to connecting so as to establish greater rapport.

LET'S RECAP

The Power of Rapport establishes a level of trust and friendship that is necessary for people to feel comfortable buying. Both Denny O. and Paul could magically connect and bond with buyers when other salespeople couldn't. Sales superstars have the Midas touch when it comes to making their buyers feel understood and believing that the salesperson is comfortable in their world. You can, too, if you connect, contact, and prompt buyers the same way the pros do.

Rapport is established by connecting with the buyer on as many levels as possible, beginning with common ground and similarities. Caring about their well-being and being flexible in your communication approach, along with being likeable and humorous, also create a bond.

What you do in the first 30 seconds of an initial contact with a buyer can either set the stage for great rapport or terminate the sales process entirely. Following a set of rules for face-to-face and telephone engagement gives you the edge to build rapport.

Becoming a state prompter means that you leverage your rapport to induce the buyer to purchase. Use your own supercharged selling state to lead buyers into their own state of passion and be ready for them to insist on your product.

Remember when matching paint was an art form? Homeowners took sample chips to the hardware store, and the proprietor would mix various colors through trial and error until satisfied that they matched. Sometimes the homeowner ended up happy with how the paint looked on the wall and sometimes not.

Today, modern hardware stores have computers that analyze paint chips. Through a complex refractory evaluation of the combined pigments in the sample chip, the computer sorts through millions of possibilities and always comes up with the same result: a perfect match. No matter what the color is, the computer matches it perfectly every time.

Sales superstars do the same. No matter what the buyer's makeup or experience, the sales pro adapts until a match is found, connection is established, and rapport can be built. When buyers feel comfortable, they can be prompted and led toward purchase.

Influence psychology is real magic, traceable directly to the fourth strand on a selling pro's DNA, the Power of Rapport.

THE POWER OF RESOURCE MANAGEMENT

Utilize Your Primary Tools to Score More Sales

You can want to be successful, and you can even want success for the right reasons. But if you don't apply the right resources, you still won't make it.
—GEORGE LUDWIG

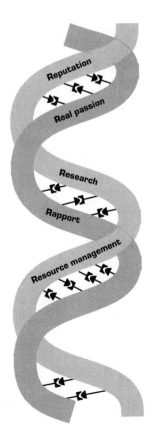

Reputation

Real passion

Research

Rapport

Resource management

Kyle W., who sold diagnostic imaging equipment in the hospital market, was frustrated in his attempts to meet a particular CEO at one of the nation's largest teaching hospitals. This guy had boxed him out of a large order and made himself completely unavailable to all salespeople. Instead of giving up, Kyle turned to his creativity and wit and developed a new approach. He dropped off a leading business book at the CEO's office in which he had highlighted passages that pertained to a particular leadership challenge the hospital was facing. In addition, he got three other area hospital leaders to write letters to this executive touting Kyle's reputation, character, and integrity.

Several days later, Kyle received a call from the CEO's assistant requesting a meeting to learn more about him, his company, and his products. Bingo! Kyle's creative ideas were so novel and compelling that they had gained him access to an intimidating, C-level executive. His application of the Power of Resource Management led to closing more than $22 million in sales revenue from that account alone and helped him finish number one that year. Kyle W.'s creativity scored a sales touchdown.

Great football coaches achieve great success by managing their resources wisely. They often must take the team that's been given them and figure out how to develop it into a powerhouse. To accomplish this, they use four primary tools. First, they *develop a game plan* that strategically builds on their team's strengths and targets opponents' weaknesses. In addition, they must always *watch the clock* to be aware of how much time is left. Then, they must *be creative* with new offensive and defensive approaches, constantly adapting their lineup to changing situations. Finally, in front of the cameras at postgame press conferences and interviews, great coaches must know how to *present themselves as winners*. Outstanding coaches use these four resources to score one touchdown after another.

Sales superstars excel in their management of the same four resources. They know that a strategic game plan that covers every aspect of their business for the year, the quarter, the month, the week, and even the day is indispensable for achieving success. Top pros are creative in their approach to every facet of selling, from marketing themselves to securing referrals to presenting their products. They also know that the most precious resource they have to trade is their time and that how they present their solution to the buyer can make or break a sale.

These tools are overriding cardinal resources, because they contain the ability to ignite the other six *Power Selling* strategies. Your *game plan, watching the clock, creativity,* and *presenting to win* leverage all of your sales efforts to drive you into the end zone for a sales TD. There you'll experience the thrill of victory, not the agony of defeat.

YOUR GAME PLAN—THE KEY TO WINNING

Imagine an NFL coach gathering his team for a pregame meeting and giving instructions like, "Don't forget to wear your helmet! Make sure to pass the ball only to the blue-and-orange jerseys. And remember, only 11 of you guys out there on the field at one time!" What would that team's chances for success be with that kind of game plan? Zero!

NFL coaches and their staff develop a strategic game plan for every single game, whether it's the preseason opener or the Super Bowl. They watch miles of game film of the opposing team, and they analyze their own players' assets and liabilities. They pore over statistics and then pull all their analysis together into a strategic game plan. This plan includes player choices, play selections, offensive and defensive formations, and even contingency options if the original plan doesn't pan out. The specific initiatives and tactical maneuvers spring from the strategic game plan.

Fortune 100 CEOs never run onto the business playing field without a thoroughly thought-out business plan, and neither do the selling elite. The concept of strategy *(strategos)* originated in ancient Greece and meant preparing and setting up forces *before the battle* commences; the tactics *(tacktikos)* used *during the battle* came from this plan. Likewise, to be successful in sales, strategic planning must precede tactical maneuvering. Sales masters know that a great strategic business plan, which comes before the actual selling, will position them in front of the right buyers at the right time with the right business solution.

Research confirms that fewer than 10 percent of salespeople have a business plan to follow and an established sales process as their daily guide. What do you think happens when you have no business plan and no proven process to implement that plan? With no clear sense of direction, you may end up heading off in all directions at once, which will definitely *not* get you closer to success.

Life Plan

Just as specific tactics come from a strategic plan, a strong business plan flows from an overall life plan. Sales success happens when your life is consistently directed by your purpose and core values. The well-defined sense of purpose we discuss in Chapter 2 does more than build a strong psychological foundation; it also directs every business decision you make. To be productive in selling, you also need to be productive when you're *not* selling. Problems in your personal life will eventually sabotage your sales results, too. As Zig Ziglar always said, "If you're hurting anywhere, you're hurting everywhere!"

Entire books have been written about how to develop a life plan, and it's beyond the scope of this book to tackle the specifics. I do want to stress the importance, though, of having something written down that defines your purpose. (See my example in Appendix A.) Commit to following some kind of life-planning, time-management system, such as FranklinCovey, Microsoft Outlook, or Anthony Robbins's Rapid Planning Method. You can also study several systems and create your own customized program. This kind of life planning, as described by Covey, helps you focus more consistently on what's truly important, as opposed to just what's urgent. Life planning and life balance lead to long-term sales success and happiness.

Strategic Business Plan

Average salespeople don't plan to fail; they just fail to plan. An NFL coach's number-one goal for the season is to win the Super Bowl. From that visionary goal, they set a goal for each game, which is simply to win that game. From this goal springs a strategic plan for each game. The top selling pros develop strategic business plans by identifying where they want their business to be at the end of a specific time frame. They start with their visionary big goals, then plan their strategic initiatives. With those initiatives in place, they set their short-range and mid-range goals and then, most importantly, plan their time.

Big goals must be simple and prioritized. You can have many sales goals, but they all should fall under a couple of big goals. For the auto salesperson, it might simply be the number of units sold or gross dollar volume. For the real estate salesperson, it might be the total dollar volume sold or total dollar volume listed, or both. For the corporate salesperson, it might be exceeding the company's quota or reaching a certain income level. No matter what the specific major business goals are, they must be clear and obvious.

> *Remember, a goal without a number is just a slogan.*
> **—JACK CANFIELD**

Your business plan should also be married to a specific time frame that's relevant for your business. A three-year window often is an ideal long-term time frame to consider for vision-planning purposes. Most salespeople never look beyond one year, but if you don't know where you want to be in three to five years, how will you get there? For specific initiatives, the one-year business plan is the primary blueprint. From a one-year plan, you can easily formulate your quarterly plans, monthly plans, and weekly scheduling.

Strategic business plans vary greatly, depending on the company you work for and the clientele you serve, but every plan must include a market position assessment, sales volume goals, filling the sales funnel, sales funnel management, client retention, and administrative duties.

Market position assessment. A sales-driven business plan must take into account the market position of any product or service. While the fundamentals of selling are the same across all industries, a product's position in terms of its life cycle, market superiority, and market momentum influences the premises upon which your business plan is founded.

When you have a clearly superior market position, your business plan should call for frontal tactics. Geoffrey Moore's book, *Inside the Tornado,* points out that in this situation, you must show the product as often and as early as possible to as many prospects as possible. Pfizer employed this strategy with phenomenal success in 1998 when they introduced Viagra® for erectile dysfunction. With no competition, they promoted their product relentlessly, until it became part of household daily language and sold millions of units.

Conversely, when your product or service doesn't enjoy such an advantage, you must formulate a different business plan. Maybe your plan can focus on selling your product to a small, specific niche, to gain a foothold where your competitors are absent. One of Betco's (Jan-San supplies) sales reps focused primarily on selling to school systems, because in his territory, the competitor dominated all other arenas. By zeroing in on school systems first, he was able to penetrate his territory successfully, gain a foothold of satisfied references, and then have enough presence to take on the more established competitor head-to-head in other arenas. In either case, a realistic market position assessment drives the plan.

Sales volume goals. Remember from Chapter 2 that focusing on your goals activates the RAS of the brain and helps create the conviction to reach the goals. Your sales volume goals direct your mental focus and form the core of your business plan.

Several elements make up your sales volume goals, the first of which is identifying your company's sales quota for you. Is it realistic, or is it too high or too low? It's better to change that number at the beginning of the fiscal year than one month before year's end. If your current market position assessment suggests that your quota is unrealistic, document your opinion objectively—don't emotionally cry that your number is just too high.

The second element is identifying your income goal. How much money do you want to make?

The third element is identifying the sales volume necessary to exceed your company's sales quota and/or your income goal. These sales volume goals should be established for the year, quarter, month, and even week, if appropriate. Sales volume goals can also be broken down by product, market, or other meaningful segment.

Filling the sales funnel. The pipeline that contains all of the prospects and buyers you currently pursue can be conceptualized best as a giant funnel. Floating above the funnel are all those prospects with whom you've never made contact. The potential buyers you've had direct contact with are just inside the big, wide top of the funnel. As the funnel narrows, the family history you've collected reduces the number of prospects. These leads are further reduced when you diagnose—you effectively *weed out* prospects to whom you're not likely to sell. Finally, down at the narrow bottom of the funnel, you have just the *hot ones*, those best few buyers whose orders are imminent. The sales funnel will be examined closely in the next section as a primary tool for managing your time, but for now, simply recognize that your overall sales success depends on how many quality leads (ideal buyers) you drop into your funnel.

Your business plan must include a detailed strategy for generating enough leads to fill your funnel and reach your sales volume goals. You know from Chapter 3 that you must first identify your *ideal buyer*, develop a *target list* of ideal buyers, and determine the appropriate *strategy* to reach them. For most industries, setting appointments by telephone, covered in Chapter 4, is the primary prospecting method and keeps the funnel full. Your personal marketing strategy (which may include advance marketing, in-person marketing, or Headliner marketing tactics) and

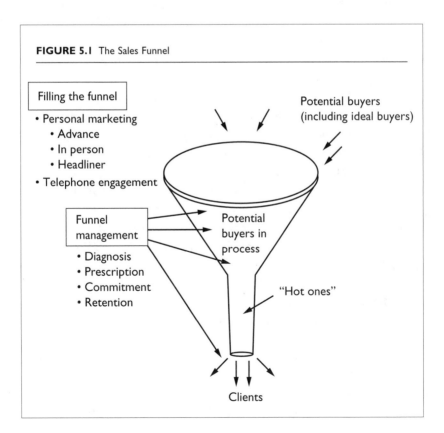

FIGURE 5.1 The Sales Funnel

Filling the funnel
- Personal marketing
  - Advance
  - In person
  - Headliner
- Telephone engagement

Potential buyers
(including ideal buyers)

Funnel management
- Diagnosis
- Prescription
- Commitment
- Retention

Potential buyers in process

"Hot ones"

Clients

your referral, networking (using your advocate list), and cold-calling initiatives should also be included in your plan.

All your initiatives should be written down and tied to specific, measurable milestones. For example, you might track the number of telephone prospecting calls attempted, referrals secured, direct-mail pieces sent out, or networking functions attended. These specific milestones, when attained, provide a high level of confidence that your sales volume goals will be reached.

Sales funnel management.
Your strategic business plan must also include specific guidelines to prioritize and handle each potential buyer at every level of your sales funnel. Determine who gets the highest priority and what steps are needed to progress to the next stage in the funnel.

Managing your sales funnel also helps you forecast—most companies are sticklers for forecasting—and successfully predict future business. When you establish key milestones at each level of the sales process, you can more easily balance short-term prospecting activity to fill the funnel with long-term management. This helps eliminate giving your sales manager "blue sky" forecasts at the end of each quarter or month.

Client retention.
This part of your business plan addresses how you will retain your clients. How will you not only meet, but exceed, their expectations? Remember from Chapter 1 that focusing on serving builds a strong reputation and that selling to a new buyer is *seven* times more expensive than selling to an existing one. Part of your business plan must include the strategies for turning clients into long-term collaborative partners. Because this is absolutely mandatory for joining the ranks of the selling elite, we have devoted Chapter 7, "The Power of Relationships," to addressing it.

Administrative duties.
This is a small but important part of any effective business plan. You must include your expense budget, paperwork requirements, forecasting reports, and any other helpful tactics that your company requires or you believe are necessary.

Great NFL coaches and sales superstars alike know that winning requires developing and following a strategic game plan. Here are a couple of Power Boosters to help you develop your business plan.

POWER BOOSTERS

- Go back to Chapter 1 and complete the Power Booster for discovering your purpose and write it down, if you haven't done so yet.

- Investigate various life-planning systems with the intent of adopting one or improving yours if you already have one.

- Develop a strategic business plan that incorporates all six components listed in this section.

- Go score some serious sales touchdowns with your new or improved plan!

WATCH THE CLOCK— DON'T LET TIME RUN OUT

In 1965, the Chicago Bears trailed the Minnesota Vikings by six points with less than two minutes to go. A running back by the name of Gale Sayers took the kickoff on the Bears's four-yard line, headed up the middle, cut to the left, ducked back to the right and scampered for the sideline. Once he reached the sideline, it was clear sailing all the way into the end zone. Nobody touched him. He scored a touchdown. A few plays later, a middle linebacker by the name of Dick Butkus grabbed an interception. On the Bears's very first play after Dick's interception, Gale Sayers scored his fourth touchdown of the day. The Bears won 45 to 37. Gale Sayers and the Bears knew that time was their scarcest resource and that they had to make every second count to win the game.

Sales superstars also know that if you don't manage time as your most precious resource, you'll remain on the bench. Starters know exactly how much time is left on the clock and use their seconds accordingly.

If you don't implement some kind of plan for effective time management, both in life and in sales, you will not become a sales superstar, and you'll probably end up unhappy and unfulfilled. You must learn to leverage the time you've devoted to selling to score more sales touchdowns.

Old time-management theory had salespeople believe it was somehow wrong not to call on every single buyer in their territory. This practice sends too many salespeople calling on too many accounts, which results in too few accounts being diagnosed properly, which results in too few orders. Remember from Chapter 2 that salespeople typically have only around 200 days per year to generate results. You *have* to make those days count if you want to become a sales superstar. A major key to sales success is spending your limited time with the best potential buyers in your universe, and three major steps help achieve this. You must *identify your ideal sales day, concentrate on your critical few,* and *work the sales funnel* for sales success.

The Ideal Sales Day

When our company is hired to develop a customized sales process and training program for a particular organization, one of the first things we try to identify is what their ideal sales day looks like. This isn't a description of the day when a salesperson brings home big orders—that's the "perfect sales day." Cha-ching! We want to identify the type of day in which you spend your time with ideal buyers, and increase the likelihood that the perfect sales day will more likely occur. Detailing this day sets a benchmark towards which you can work as you conduct your weekly planning and execute your daily tasks.

We create a descriptive template, based upon the company's sales team's input, that identifies what activities—if performed every day— would result in moving the sales efforts of the territory forward in the fastest manner.

The best way to show how the ideal sales day is formulated is to give examples. For Betco, we identified the ideal sales day as a day in which the salesperson visited two or more ideal buyers from their target account list, completed the precall identification research (i.e., the family history), and wrote up an account strategy for each call. When Betco sales personnel planned their days to line up closely with this ideal sales day, they increased their sales results, and the company's management team had greater confidence about hitting their year-end quota.

For Johnson & Johnson's Advance Sterilization Products (ASP) division, an ideal sales day occurred when a sales specialist called on three or more ideal buyers (hospitals) from their target account list. An ideal buyer for ASP included (but was not limited to) hospitals that have good financial health, expanding surgical procedures, archaic sterilization equipment, and easy access to all buying influences. The ideal sales day also included engaging four or more contacts at each hospital and gathering all the buying influences together for a single meeting. Each meeting would be conducted from precall research, which was included in a written account call strategy.

Every sales master, and every world-class selling organization, must identify their ideal sales day so they can benchmark their time management. This ensures that they spend their most precious resource—their time—with the prospects who are most likely to make them the happiest—the ones who purchase their products.

Concentrate on Your Critical Few

Vilfredo Pareto, an Italian economist, observed in the early 1900s that 20 percent of the Italian people owned 80 percent of their country's wealth. Over time and through rigorous application to many fields of study and business, his principle has become accepted as a valid premise regarding the relationship between input and output. His theory, called Pareto's Principle or the 80/20 Rule, states that 20 percent of all possible inputs for any given task will create 80 percent of the outputs, or results.

How does this rule apply to selling? Twenty percent of the total activities you engage in will result in 80 percent of your sales results. That 20 percent of activities (which vary by industry, product, marketplace, time of year, your current situation, and even the competition) are your best practices, your *critical few*. Identifying and concentrating on the critical few every single day help you manage your limited time and lead to sales success.

Never begin the day until it is finished on paper.
—JIM ROHN

Jim Meisenheimer, a sales strategist from Lakewood Ranch, Florida, starts every day with a six-pack. Not beer—he recommends starting every selling day by listing the six most important things to be completed that day and then working from the list.

You must also analyze and identify which of your current activities are total time wasters. Get rid of them, or clump them together in your schedule—or, better yet, delegate them. Make a serious attempt to minimize administrative paperwork and then complete it during the hours you're normally least productive. Schedule your face-to-face and telephone engagement during the time you're likely to be in your peak state. Use your drive time for continuing education by listening to audio programs. Learn to say "no" more often by not dropping everything and running after buyers who definitely do not fit your ideal buyer profile. Acquire any productivity boosters like contact-management software, a cell phone, pager, PDA, or other tool that minimizes your time away from the critical few activities that produce your best results.

Work the Sales Funnel

In 1967, I rode my first big roller coaster. I screamed with joy and hung on for dear life as we plunged several hundred feet toward the finish of the Blue Streak at Cedar Point in Sandusky, Ohio. I fell in love with the rush of speed and adrenaline from roller coasters and still think they're awesome fun for young and old alike.

In 1985, I rode a different kind of roller coaster. I sold defibrillators for a division of Eli Lilly and enjoyed a huge first quarter, followed by a second quarter dump, followed by a modest climb in the third quarter, followed by another plunge. This roller-coaster ride was no fun at all. I had big commissions one quarter but had to eat at fast food joints and deal with an angry sales manager the next.

I've since learned that the roller-coaster effect in sales comes from letting your sales funnel run dry, which means that sooner or later, you'll have a dry wallet, too. Ouch! Most salespeople (including me in 1985) prospect like crazy when they discover that their funnels are empty. But the time lag between prospecting and actual sales creates a roller-coaster sales effect.

Sales superstars, on the other hand, prioritize their selling time differently so that their funnel stays full, their wallet stays full, and their ride is smooth. Top selling professionals know how to work the sales funnel to manage their time and prioritize their selling tasks.

Growing up in Indiana gave me the opportunity to learn a few lessons about life and managing a sales funnel by studying the neighboring farmers.

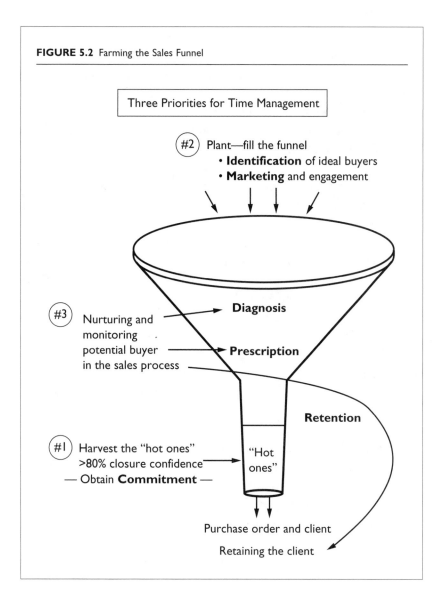

FIGURE 5.2 Farming the Sales Funnel

The first law of the farm states that when your crop is ready, you must harvest it. Farmers often run their combines long after sundown, using headlights to help them see in the dark. They put in the long hours because crops left in the field will spoil. Top salespeople prioritize their time so that the *number-one priority* item on their *critical few* list is devoted to *obtaining commitment* from potential buyers who are ready to "harvest"—the *hot ones* in the sales funnel. These potential buyers have at least an 80 percent confidence level for purchasing. They have agreed with your diagnosis and they see *your* solution. You have confirmed that your prescription is the right one. These opportunities should always be your number-one time priority because they guarantee a steady sales and income stream. If they're left alone, they too will spoil or, worse, be harvested by your competitor. Most salespeople—from rookie to pro—do in fact make this their highest priority.

The second law of the farm states that if you don't plant seed, you're not going to get a crop. Your *number-two priority* for time management, for most industries and sales positions, is to "plant" your buyers. Rookies don't plant, and that's why they get a sparse harvest.

If you don't put viable prospects into your sales funnel, you won't get any sales flowing out the bottom. The number of leads you put into your funnel at any given time directly relates to the number of sales you'll enjoy later. Farming is also long term. You can't plant in September and get a crop in October; you must plant in April to get a crop in October. Same thing is true in sales. You must put viable leads into your funnel long before you expect sales results to avoid the dreaded rollercoaster effect. Always plant—always fill your funnel with *ideal buyers*—as your second priority.

The third law of the farm requires that the farmer continually monitor the seedlings and nurture them toward maturity for harvest. The farmer regularly fertilizes, uses insecticide, removes weeds, and waters the crop all summer long. Sales masters monitor and nurture every potential buyer in their funnels as their *number-three time management priority.* This means finishing the family history (identification), performing the thorough assessment (diagnosis), presenting the solution (prescription), and building a repeat client relationship (retention).

The key is to identify which critical few activities (best practices), based on your business, move the buyer forward through the funnel toward commitment.

Working your sales funnel effectively requires following the three laws of the farm to prioritize how you spend your time. First spend time with the hot prospects that are ready to commit to purchase, next fill your funnel, and finally nurture the potential buyers in your funnel.

NFL coaches, players, and all sales pros watch the clock so time doesn't get away from them. Knowing what your ideal sales day looks like, concentrating on your *critical few* activities, and working the sales funnel will have you scoring touchdown after touchdown long before the two-minute warning sounds. Here are several Power Boosters to maximize your most precious resource—time.

POWER BOOSTERS

- Determine your ideal sales day and try to plan next week (and the weeks to come) around that model.

- Determine the critical few activities for every level in your sales funnel.

- Commit to being not just a Doctor of Selling but a farmer, too— always be planting and filling your sales funnel.

- Remember the three laws of the farm. Close the hot ones first. Fill your funnel second. Nurture the rest third.

CREATIVITY—THINK OUTSIDE THE PLAYBOOK

Bill Parcells has coached four different NFL football teams, including the championship New York Giants. Bill is famous for always having a trick play or unorthodox spread up his sleeve to get his team into the end zone fast. These ideas were not in the playbook. Coach Parcells knew that thinking outside the box—thinking outside the playbook—was a valuable resource for winning football games.

Kyle W. surprised both his superiors and his peers when he dreamed up the idea to combine his common knowledge about a hospital's challenges with a relevant business book and a few reference letters. His creative tactics secured him an entree with a high-level buyer. Competition in sales is so fierce that salespeople must be creative or risk losing the sale to someone who is.

Sales superstars from every industry develop new approaches that pay off in all facets of selling. Their creativity overcomes obstacles, presents different solutions to a problem, or develops an innovative way to generate more sales and serve buyers. Top producers work their game plan, but they know that on occasion, they must think outside the playbook and trust their gut to move a potential buyer forward creatively. Their keys to creativity are *trying new approaches* and *picking up ideas from their peers*.

Try a New Approach

In sales, the need for new ideas is always great, because the selling environment changes rapidly due to many different buyer personalities, economic conditions, complex buyer politics, emerging products, competitive activity, and a slew of other factors. Sales masters know that your past experiences, especially successful ones, can actually be a handicap if you only look to reuse these strategies. The pros know that you must constantly adapt and think *outside* the playbook, while still working *from* the playbook. Don't abandon all the smart, tried-and-true sales steps that have made you successful, but also look for innovative ideas, tactics, and plans. In short, always be willing to try something different, like Kyle did when he needed to reach that unreachable CEO.

Another example of creative selling comes from Jim P., a real estate salesperson who pioneered an innovative way to reach potential real estate buyers. He invented a novel approach for selling new condominiums that overlooked a golf course. Jim advertised a series of free golf clinics that showcased a local teaching pro and featured a prize raffle. After three clinics, Jim had accumulated a database of more than 200 local golfers. Jim then prospected those golfers by direct mail first and then by telephone follow-up (with a script). He was able to schedule 26 showings, which eventually led to 8 sales. Jim snagged close to $80,000 in sales commissions from a small investment, a little elbow grease, and a creative approach.

There are infinite new tactics that are both creative and resourceful. Remember from Chapter 1 how important it is to stand out and to focus on serving? Sending unusual sales letters, birthday cards, or thank-you notes accomplishes both. Anies H. was ingenious when he drove that Porsche over 250 miles to show it to me. That's way out of a typical auto salesperson's playbook, but it paid off—I couldn't help but buy. You can also be creative in your manner of dress, innovative with your business card design, or unique with your personal marketing brochures.

> *Nothing is so useless as general maxim.*
> **—LORD THOMAS BABINGTON MACAULAY**

You can find original ways to follow up with buyers, too. Remembering buyers' triumphs and tragedies, their children's names, and favorites sports or cultural interests can all be accomplished creatively. One Johnson & Johnson salesperson always e-mailed his top clients who followed a particular sports team a little quip from the newspaper about their team (even if it was the Chicago Cubs). His clients loved it. One real estate salesperson made it a habit to always remember her clients' pets' names. Now that's creative and resourceful!

How you present your product or service is another avenue that lends itself to creative flair, especially in positioning a product so its drawbacks are minimized. When plasma sterilization was first introduced by Johnson & Johnson, many potential buyers perceived that its small chamber was a drawback when compared to the traditional sterilizers. Even when they were told that the plasma sterilizer could process a much larger quantity of instrumentation in the same time frame, because it was faster, they still couldn't grasp the advantage. These buyers were used to evaluating sterilizers based on what they could see—the size of the chamber.

Finally, one rep developed a persuasive handout that included visual comparisons of the two systems' total output in any given day. When he showed the drawing to potential buyers, they could see that the chamber size didn't control the sterilizer's effectiveness. This new approach overcame that particular obstacle and opened up a lot of sales opportunities, despite the fact that it wasn't revolutionary—it just tweaked the existing presentation method.

These examples show the benefits of trying new strategies. I offer them not for you to copy them but to encourage you to keep trying new approaches until you unlock a sales windfall. If you want to become a sales superstar, you must think outside your playbook.

Tap Your Peers

Professional football players often pick up new strategies by poring over game tapes and observing how other players have successfully outmaneuvered an opponent. Wide receivers routinely query each other about which pass pattern route to run or which particular move—shoulders, head, hips, legs, or eye fake—will work best to blast past a particular cornerback or safety.

Sales pros also know that tapping their teammates can help develop creative new strategies. Sometimes a fellow salesperson already uses a successful approach that's new to your selling repertoire. By implementing how your colleague generated sales success, you also can become more successful.

When I first learned to sell defibrillators to the hospital market, I picked up a creative approach from a fellow salesperson named Carlos Q. Before I worked with Carlos, I generally asked the nurse buyer a few questions and then took them through a standard demonstration of the equipment. Working with Carlos opened my eyes to how a fully engaged equipment demonstration should be conducted.

After Carlos carefully asked Sally, an ICU nurse, a series of diagnostic questions (and confirmed his diagnosis), he began to reenact a "code blue" scenario, complete with all the intensity and adrenaline of a real-life cardiac arrest event. He used his simulator to re-create the V-fib heart rhythm. Then he aggressively pulled out the paddles and began responding just like a nurse or doctor would react in a life-threatening situation. Carlos set the dials, charged up the de-fib, barked the commands, and pretended to de-fib an imaginary patient. Carlos made the TV show *ER* seem almost flat-line.

Carlos went through the entire sequence a second time, but this time he insisted that Sally do all the work with the defibrillator. Carlos got her physically involved in every aspect of the demonstration, while he addressed every point she had mentioned in the diagnosis that was important to her.

Carlos's creative theatrics and method of involving Sally in the demonstration taught me that physical involvement by the prospect leads to a feeling of ownership, before they've bought anything. His innovative style, passionate state, and ability to get Sally tactilely involved with the defibrillator created greater emotional involvement by her. My observation of Carlos's unique presentation style helped me develop my own effective equipment demonstration. Thank you, Carlos Q.!

Tapping into your peers also includes synergizing with them to invent completely new methods. In every industry, regularly scheduled meetings have great value for sharing ideas, strategies, and resourceful approaches that are outside the playbook. Sales managers take heed: schedule those meetings even when you hate to take your people out of the field. Doing what's important must take precedence over doing what's urgent, if you want to enjoy sales stardom for the long haul.

Creativity can drive you into the end zone of sales results. Here are a few Power Boosters that will help you get creativity and resourcefulness back in your sales game.

POWER BOOSTERS

- List the top ten problems you face selling your product or service and set aside two hours to creatively brainstorm new approaches.

- Come up with at least one new way to market or prospect for new ideal buyers.

- Come up with at least one new way you can creatively stand out.

- Come up with at least one new way you can follow up with your best clients.

(continued)

- Identify one drawback of or objection to your product or service that has cost you sales and commit to finding a better way to present or minimize the shortcoming.

- Identify two or three sales pros whom you will call regularly and soak up every success strategy they have.

- Pressure your sales manager to schedule meetings regularly for sharing ideas and brainstorming new approaches.

PRESENT TO WIN— PRESCRIBE THE SOLUTION

During NFL postgame press conferences, coaches and players alike have learned that how they present themselves and discuss their game can dramatically affect both public opinion of their team and ticket sales.

Sales superstars also have learned that how they present the solution that their product provides is one of their primary resources for getting a sale—and a commission. The selling elite prescribe their solutions far more effectively than the rookies. They present in such a way that the potential buyer sees their solution and agrees with it.

Many sales books stress how to present your solution persuasively to the buyer, and most salespeople do so fairly well, because they're excited about their product and how it will help the buyer. The top pros, however, distinguish themselves from the rookies by the work they've done *before* presentation time—in their comprehensive identification of the problem (the family history) and clear diagnosis (the thorough assessment). They always remember not to prescribe their solution without first confirming their diagnosis—in other words, they *never present without consent*. But, even with thorough research, if the manner in which you prescribe your solution is unprofessional, or lacking, you can still blow the sale. Sales superstars *prescribe with buyer agreement* and *follow basic presentation guidelines* when it's time to talk about their product or service.

Prescribe with Buyer Agreement

Top selling professionals create a vision of *their* solution in the mind of the buyer. When buyers see and agree with this prescription, they'll usually push to close. To understand how sales superstars create this buyer agreement, it's important to distinguish among some sales definitions. Old sales training books talked about a product's *features* and *benefits*, but it's more helpful to distinguish a product's *features, advantages,* and *benefits*. These distinctions were first made popular by Neil Rackham, author of *SPIN Selling,* and Mike Bosworth, author of *Solution Selling.*

> *Describe your product in terms of what it does, not in terms of what it is.*
> **—BRIAN TRACY**

Imagine a beautiful sports car with a CD player. The *feature statement* is, "This car has a CD player." The CD player is one of the car's features. Average salespeople love to sell features. You've probably been to a car dealership where the salesperson excitedly showed you every bell and whistle (feature) on the car, most of which you could care less about. This is prescribing without tying the prescription to the needs of the buyer, which should have been determined in the diagnosis.

The *advantage statement* is, "The CD player enables you to play all kinds of great music whenever you want to." These are the statements where a salesperson describes how the buyer will either gain or eliminate pain by using the feature. Because the car has a CD player, you can enjoy great music anytime.

Most salespeople think that advantages are benefits, because they assume the advantage is a benefit for every buyer. That's where the problems arise prescribing the solution. In reality, an advantage is a benefit only if the buyer says it's important. Solutions are the accumulation of a product's *specific* benefits that are in the mind of the *buyer,* not the salesperson. If salespeople diagnose properly, they know which advantages are actually benefits for that buyer. While it's always better to share advantages than features, if the advantages don't matter to the buyer, you're just wasting air, because they're not benefits. The sports car may have a great CD player, but if the potential buyer hates music or only listens to talk radio, then it's not a benefit. Buyers listen to only one radio station when it comes to benefits and solutions—WII-FM (What's In It For Me)!

A good *benefit statement* is, "The CD player enables you to play all kinds of great music whenever you choose, which *you said* was something you wanted to be able to do." This type of statement is tying the feature to a specific benefit that the buyer has admitted wanting. If you uncover during the diagnosis that the potential buyer loves music, then that benefit should be part of the buying solution.

By doing a thorough diagnosis, you're able to *present only those benefits* that will meet the buyer's needs. When buyers agree with you about their needs and desired benefits, they'll be far more likely to agree with you about the solution. Remember that buyers don't buy products or services; they buy the *states* that they imagine they will experience after purchase. You communicate the state that they'll experience via the benefits that matter to them, and these combined benefits *form their solution.*

Research has documented that the most effective sales presentations prescribe benefits and spend very little time talking about product features. Instead of talking about the graphic equalizer in the CD player, the sales pro paints the picture of you driving down the road enjoying your favorite music. Better yet, the pro takes you for a ride and, with you driving, puts in one of your favorite CDs that you grabbed from your old car.

Magnification questions (from RPM questioning in Chapter 3) can help transport potential buyers into the future state, where they get to experience your solution's benefits. "What music do you like to listen to?" and, "What would it feel like to be cruising south on Lake Shore Drive listening to some Simon and Garfunkel?" are examples of questions for a buyer who likes Paul Simon tunes (obviously an older buyer like me). Questions can also magnify the pain of not having your solution as well. "Have you noticed how bad the music on the radio has gotten lately?" Prescribing your solution comes down to a mixture of making *benefit statements,* sharing other buyers' success stories, and leading the potential buyer with questions.

Great salespeople, when they're presenting their solution and seeking buyer agreement in competitive situations, also *differentiate.* Differentiating your product or service comes down to zeroing in on the *benefits* (advantages the buyer said were important) of your solution that offer a unique advantage. They prescribe all the benefits that the buyer said were important, but they give special attention to emphasizing those that enjoy a *differentiated superiority* over the competition. Sales superstars list all their benefits on paper, for their own reference, and make a special annotation of the differentiated ones.

A final way to increase buyer agreement is to *offer proof.* Remember that buyer suspicion is always high. After diagnosing properly, confirming that diagnosis, and prescribing the solution based on benefits the buyer acknowledged, your buyer may still feel some anxiety. Sales masters pick up on this emotion both verbally and nonverbally, and they immediately offer proof to help the buyer over the hump to committing to their solution. Product demonstrations, product trials, site visits, reference success letters or calls, the client list, a test ride, and sample pharmaceuticals are a few of the ways you can offer proof that *your solution is their best solution.*

Basic Presentation Guidelines

Effective presentations require you to draw simultaneously on many of the strategies discussed in *Power Selling.* You need *real passion* to be in your supercharged selling state and communicate your solution enthusiastically and confidently. The Power of Research, used during your identification and diagnosis, determines which benefits you stress during your presentation. The Power of Rapport is needed to connect with buyers when you prescribe your solution, so that their confidence in your prescription remains high. Strong rapport also allows you to be a *state prompter* and more easily move the buyer toward your solution.

In addition to those broad strategies, sales masters also use several specific presentation tools to win buyer commitment. They always remain professional, organized, and articulate to inspire buyer confidence. When buyers admit that they have a need during diagnosis, they often feel vulnerable and wonder if you'll try to take advantage of them. Avoid negative words or phrases that sound insincere, such as *honestly, frankly, quite frankly,* and *trust me on this one.* Your professional, expert presentation will inspire their confidence so they can comfortably move forward in the buying process.

Top sales pros share *reference success stories* during presentations so that buyers can *see* how other buyers with similar problems were helped by their solution. These stories also help buyers overcome any remaining suspicion. They are similar to the reference stories used in telephone engagement, except that now you must tell the whole story, including how the solution worked.

Salespeople need many reference success stories, categorized by product and market segment, which they can share effectively and concisely. These stories, if told expertly, should *prompt the state* of the potential buyer by tapping into the emotional need to move away from pain and toward gain. Average salespeople usually have only one or two stories, and they often can't tell them in a way that evokes emotion. These stories can also be used to *provide proof* about a benefit.

Your *client list* of satisfied clients should be made available to potential buyers. This serves as a big reputation-builder and also provides Social Proof, if the names are significant to the buyer. This list should include clients whom the buyer can call, and you should provide letters extolling your product's solutions that the buyer can review. The best option is for clients who were in the reference success stories you just shared to be available to take calls or be visited by the potential buyer. One of the most successful techniques at Johnson & Johnson's ASP division was to have potential buyers visit a reference success story account and see the solution for themselves. That's powerful presenting!

First-class presentations always involve as many of the potential buyers' senses as you can. Have things for them to look at and handle while they're listening to you. Involve their visual, auditory, or kinesthetic senses as much as possible by getting the potential buyer as physically involved in the presentation as possible. Remember how Carlos Q. got Sally to run the defibrillator, which created a feeling of ownership and emotional involvement? Physical involvement will definitely generate more sales because, as Chapter 4 demonstrated, buyer motion leads to buyer emotion and vice versa. Physical involvement also helps you discover how receptive buyers are to seeing your solution. By keenly observing their nonverbal actions during physical involvement, you can gauge their level of acceptance or resistance.

Get buyers to push the buttons, ride the floor scrubber, turn on the equipment, drive the car, walk every room of the house, handle the client list, hold the sample, leaf through the binder, assemble the part, or put the trays into the sterilizer. It's easier to get a potential buyer involved in a product purchase than a service purchase, but with a little *creativity*, you can usually find a way. You can even get buyers involved in a group presentation. Have them help with the easel, projector, or video machine. Rookie salespeople often want to show off with a whiz-bang demonstration, but this usually bores buyers because they're not involved. Physical involvement leads to emotional involvement, which leads toward purchase.

A final presentation guideline is for presenting to a group of potential buyers and influencers at one time. If possible, meet with every attendee prior to your presentation and conduct a thorough assessment. This gives you the advantage both of establishing rapport and of being able to zero in on the key points that address their true needs. Prepare written objectives for your presentation. What do you hope to accomplish?

To begin the presentation, have someone else introduce you, if possible. Try to leverage the first three minutes for building rapport and credibility. Use your reference success stories as much as possible and get the audience involved. Remember not to take yourself too seriously. Close the presentation with a summary of the benefits they agreed to and enthusiastically call them to action.

NFL coaches and sales superstars all recognize that how they present themselves and their products greatly influences their reception. Sales pros prescribe their solution with buyer agreement and winning guidelines. Here are your Power Boosters for first-class presentations.

POWER BOOSTERS

- Understand and memorize the difference between features, advantages, and benefits.

- Develop a list of all your benefits (those features that your buyers have said are benefits) and a list of differentiated and unique benefits for your products.

- Develop a repertoire of handy proof sources to help buyers get over the anxiety hump.

- Utilize passion, research, and rapport to form the foundation for presenting your solution.

(continued)

- Develop at least one reference success story for every major product solution.

- Absolutely have a printed client list and several testimonial letters from satisfied clients.

- Present your product involving as many buyer senses (visual, auditory, and kinesthetic) as you can, and get the buyer as physically involved in the demonstration as possible.

LET'S RECAP

All great football coaches and sales superstars use their resources wisely. Mike Ditka, Kyle W., and the selling elite utilize their primary tools—a strategic business plan, time management, creativity, and presentation skills—to score more sales.

Developing a strategic game plan for your business and managing your time are critical if you want to get into the end zone of sales success. Selling without a game plan and failing to watch the clock are like squaring off against former Bears defensive lineman Richard Dent without a helmet and pads. Ouch—that's going to hurt! Being willing to think outside the playbook by trying new approaches and tapping into your peer network will feed you those innovative, game-winning plays for which Bill Parcells is known. NFL coaches and top producers both use great presentations to win over fans and secure a sale.

Imagine being in the locker room at the halftime of your sales year when you're getting tromped. Your sales results stink, your spirit is broken, your funnel appears empty, and your future looks bleak. Beads of perspiration begin to trickle down your face. Your chest feels tight, and panic is beginning to set in. Your mission: to turn things around! You have no other sales players you can call in, no marketing budget, and no "give me" sales to turn around your sales game.

What do you do?

It's time to get inspired by the master of resource management—MacGyver! The lead character of the television series by the same name,

MacGyver was the miracle man of resource management. He reversed seemingly hopeless scenarios by creatively using whatever's available. He has been known to make a parabolic mirror from the remains of a blown-up jeep. He has found household items to build a simple radio that rescues him and saves the day. MacGyver always managed his resources to win the day. Ingenious, resourceful, always with a plan, cognizant of time constraints, and able to persuade others with his solutions—MacGyver is the man to clone. His DNA has the Power of Resource Management on its fifth strand, and it can win the day for you, too.

6

THE POWER OF RESILIENCY

Turn Setbacks into Comebacks

It is not whether you get knocked down; it's whether you get back up.
—VINCE LOMBARDI

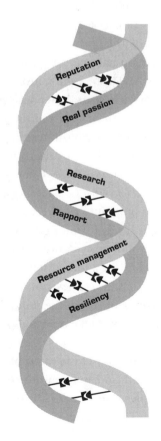

John Abdo invented a revolutionary fitness device for strengthening the abdominal core and spinal muscle groups. He tried to sell the device for several years, giving hundreds of presentations and trying a TV test run that failed. Everyone told John to shelve his idea. He was well over $100,000 in debt and had heard the word *no* hundreds of times. But John had the Power of Resiliency. Despite the obstacles, the adversities, and the fears, he never stopped believing in and fighting for his product and his dream. John knew that no great product ever becomes successful until someone commits to selling it with relentless determination. John just kept selling!

Completely broke, John moved to California and started selling his idea again. He made call after call. He enlisted the help of every agent and contact he knew. They, too, made call after call. He prayed for God's help. After six months in California and within days of bankruptcy, John continued the calls that are necessary to turn setbacks into comebacks. One sales presentation finally led to a new infomercial pilot showcasing John and his product live on national TV. John's resiliency paid off like winning the lotto! The AB-DOer, John's invention, brought in more than $300 million in its first two years. When I asked John how he turned it around, he said, "By my faith in God and the fact that giving up was never an option." John's story demonstrates the Power of Resiliency— the ability to keep bouncing back from adversity.

Speaker and best-selling author Roger Crawford describes the Power of Resiliency in his book, *How High Can You Bounce?* He points out that if you take a golf ball and put it into the freezer, it will lose its resilience. No matter how hard you hit it, it won't go very far. If it's frozen cold enough, it will shatter upon impact. A normal golf ball, however, has a very flexible core and will fly for a long distance when it's hit hard.

Salespeople are like that, too. They can look alike, talk alike, and work in the very same company. Yet in the same situation, one will soar and another will shatter. One will take rejection or frustration and flourish; another will be devastated. Those salespeople who soar use the Power of Resiliency. They transform the many blows that every salesperson experiences into speed and momentum toward more sales. The same adversity that cripples one salesperson becomes a major driving force for sales superstars. They get up off the mat, they get back in the ring, and they keep turning setbacks into comebacks. The Power of Resiliency breeds the persistence and tenacity that's needed to become a superstar in the sport of selling.

How do you become resilient? Well, the good news is that you already are. To just show up in life, you had to be stronger, more persistent, and more tenacious than 16 million other sperm who competed against you. You closed the sale of a lifetime—the chance to participate in life! You chose sales as an endeavor. This is not a profession for the wimps, whiners, and worriers of the world. So congratulations are definitely in order for showing some resilience already!

Only a few sales pros seem to be naturally blessed with boundless resilience, jumping for joy no matter how many times they get rejected, objected to, or told, "You'll never make it." Maybe you've met a couple of these folks—they're definitely a strange breed! Most top selling pros, though, have had to work at building enough resiliency to reach that special destination known as sales stardom.

Sales superstars are like pilots when it comes to dealing with adversity. Pilots constantly face difficulties and unexpected obstacles when they fly. Gravity tries to prevent them from taking off, wind pushes them off course, airspace restrictions cause them to alter their course, mechanical system breakdowns create havoc, weather causes turbulence, and unexpected air traffic can alter their plans. Additionally, crosswind landings, night flying, instrument landing approaches, and emergency procedures all present challenges even for veteran airline captains.

Selling has its share of obstacles and setbacks, too. Significant rejection, call reluctance fear, unethical clients, buyer objections, competitor activity, changing bosses, changing territories, and company mergers all hinder the salesperson. Having to be an expert in selling strategy, time management, product knowledge, and industry news 200 days per year is not an easy undertaking. An increasingly complex and sophisticated marketplace, which includes a trend toward rapid commoditization of products and services, makes sales efforts more challenging than at any time in history. In addition, buyers work harder than ever to devalue the differences between products and services so that they can reduce their decision to the lowest common denominator—the selling price. It's just not easy out there!

But, as tough as it is, you can still win, just like John Abdo did. You can join the ranks of the selling elite who overcame adversity to succeed.

You have a choice. You can master how to fly out of the gravitational pull of lackluster results and climb into the sky of stellar sales numbers. You can navigate right through the turbulence of all the challenges described above. You can take off and fly away from a long, drawn-out sales slump like an F-16 jet blasts away from the deck of an aircraft carrier. And you can enjoy a beautiful, tire-screeching landing on the airstrip known as sales stardom.

Pilots follow three steps to become resilient enough to handle the adversity that comes with flying in tough conditions. First, they accept and even anticipate that difficulties like rough weather and mechanical breakdowns are part and parcel of flying. Second, they use their attitude indicator to keep them on course to their final destination. And third, they never give up—they know the flight's not over until they land.

Sales superstars must follow the same three steps. They accept that rejection, lost sales, company politics, manufacturing foul-ups, and other setbacks are part of every selling day. They also know that their attitude will carry them through any turbulence in their career. Finally, they know that their journey is not complete until they stroll down the red carpet to collect their "Sales Oscar." In short, top sales producers develop resiliency by knowing the following:

- Sales is not the big easy.
- Use your attitude indicator.
- It's not over until you win.

SALES IS NOT THE BIG EASY— ACCEPT THE TURBULENCE

Learning to fly teaches some great lessons in developing resiliency. Unlike early flyer Cal Rogers, who flew the *Vin Fizz* on the first transcontinental flight in 1911 and whose training by the Wright school in Dayton, Ohio, lasted only 90 minutes, my pilot training lasted over 12 months. What I learned was designed to save my life if I got in trouble, and I've used my lessons a few times. Now that's motivation to learn!

Part of learning to fly is accepting the discomfort of those bucks, bumps, and bounces in the atmosphere commonly called *air pockets*. Turbulence is caused by thermals, rising columns of air kicked up by the sun's uneven heating of the Earth's surface. To a passenger climbing out after takeoff in a Boeing 777, flying through "light turbulence" is a mild annoyance, but in a Cessna 172, it can be hair raising. The airplane feels like it's on the edge of falling out of control as something tries to knock it right out of the sky.

Over time, I have learned to accept the turbulence I once feared— it's part of the wonderful experience called flying. Through the slow process of acclimatizing myself to turbulence—making repeated steep turns, learning to fly under a hood with no view of the outside or the horizon, using only instruments to keep the airplane straight and level—I've been able to overcome my fear of falling from the sky. By accepting adversity and facing it every day, you become more resilient in handling it well.

In Scott Peck's best-selling book *The Road Less Traveled*, the very first sentence reads, "Life is difficult." Dr. Peck was referring to life in general, but he certainly could have been writing specifically about sales. This is an important truth, because once you understand this wisdom regarding adversity, you begin to rise above it. Paradoxically, once you know that sales is tough—once you accept that the flight to sales stardom is a turbulent one—then sales is no longer quite as difficult.

> *Life is pain, princess. And anybody who tries to tell you differently*
> *is selling something.*
> **—WESLEY, IN *THE PRINCESS BRIDE***

Average salespeople don't fully accept that selling is tough. They believe that sales should not be such a struggle and that most challenges they face are beyond their control. They'll tell you, and anybody else who will listen, why they haven't made it big or why they haven't made it at all. They'll whine, worry, and wimp out every chance they get. They'll moan and groan about the economy or their products, territory, competitors, boss, colleagues, buyers, or any other aspect of selling for which they can blame their lack of success. They act as if sales *should be* easy. News flash: *Sales is not the big easy.* If you want the big easy, head to New Orleans and party; *that's* the big easy!

Selling is a series of challenges. Do you want to whine about them or overcome them? The only way to become a sales superstar is simply to accept that adversity is part of the program and then *decide* that you will not only persevere, you will *prevail.* You cannot overcome the challenges of selling except by overcoming the challenges of selling. The truth of that statement lies in the conscious decision to commit yourself to accepting both the inevitable adversity and the responsibility to rise above it. Research investigating thousands of people who have survived traumatic events has demonstrated that these two factors determined whether they gave up or managed not only to survive but thrive.

> *The price of greatness is responsibility.*
> **—WINSTON CHURCHILL**

Julie R., a real estate salesperson whom I coached, complained that her business was way off because the local real estate market was soft (which it was). She worked very hard, but she also whined every day about the marketplace. How do you think her whining was affecting her state? Did she leave the house every day in her supercharged selling state? Hardly! She had accepted the adversity of a flat market, but she had not accepted that the adversity was *her* challenge to overcome.

She also had not identified her ideal buyer type and didn't have a solid marketing and telephone engagement plan (with script) in place that would fill her funnel with high-quality leads. She usually devoted only a few calls per day to finding new business and then bagged it. She had tried a direct mailing but had only gotten one lead.

"Nobody's buying. It's not *me,"* she said exasperatedly.

What Julie didn't understand was that she had yet to accept that her adversity was *her* challenge to overcome. Sales superstars take responsibility; they accept the fact that the adversity they face is *theirs* and nobody else's. The top pros agree with Ward Cleaver, from the television show *Leave It to Beaver,* who used to say, "You're either part of the solution, or you're part of the problem."

When I'm flying, I can't stop Mother Nature from creating the thermals that cause turbulence. Turbulence is just part of flying. That doesn't mean that I fly through some "heavy chop" grinning ear-to-ear, but it does mean that I know my job is to cope and that I won't blame someone else for how I react. My training has prepared me to change altitudes, change speeds, change routes, land and wait the weather out, or bounce along like a cowboy trying to break in a new stallion. I'll do whatever's needed to make it!

Top selling pros know that turbulence is just part of sales, too. They rely on their training and *Power Selling* strategies to prepare them for any "course adjustments" that are needed. They don't expect sales to be easy or that others will solve their problems for them. Superstars take on their challenges with gusto and forge ahead.

A great story of resiliency comes from Rudy Garcia-Tolson. Although Rudy is not in sales, his testimony inspires all of us. He was born in 1988 with a cadre of challenges. Rudy had rare, multiple birth defects: leg-crippling pterygium syndrome, a club foot, webbed fingers, and a cleft lip and palate. Rudy underwent 15 surgeries by the time he was five years old to correct the deformities, but he still couldn't walk. His hopes, and those of his parents, hit rock bottom.

At the age of five, Rudy was left with only one option. When the orthopedic surgeon asked if he was ready to have his deformed legs amputated, he responded courageously, "Cut 'em off." Years later, Rudy would say, "I was little and it was hard to face, but I knew it was the right choice." Rudy's dad said, "Rudy went to hell and back."

One month later, Rudy was fitted with new prostheses, and several months later, he walked for the first time. Rudy began his quest not just to survive but thrive. Today he can run, swim, skateboard, lift weights, and play just like any fun-loving kid. Rudy showed the resiliency to turn tragedy into triumph.

Rudy began running at age seven, and while he may be just one of many faces in a typical 5K race, two things set him apart: the steely resolve in his eyes and the flashing steel of his prosthetic legs. In 2000, he posted times for the mile of 7:20 and, for the 5K, 27:50. Pretty incredible! Rudy is one of the very few double-amputee children who can run more than a few steps. And, as if that weren't amazing enough, Rudy is also a championship swimmer. He's the youngest swimmer ever to receive the gold medal, at age six, in the 1999 Swimming Disability Championships for the 200-meter breaststroke.

In 2000, Rudy competed in more than 25 road races, 20 swim meets, 10 triathlon relays, and his first solo triathlon. Rudy—the prince of resiliency—has become one of America's leading ambassadors for physically challenged children. Rudy teaches all of us that we are greater than any challenge or problem we will ever face.

Before we explore how to form that protective shield of resiliency, here are a few Power Boosters to help you accept the adversity inherent in selling.

POWER BOOSTERS

• Acknowledge that selling is not easy, but realize that you are greater than any challenge you will face.

• Decide to take full responsibility, from this point forward, for every challenge and setback.

• Decide that you will triumph over every sales setback on your way to sales stardom!

USE YOUR ATTITUDE INDICATOR— HANDLING THE TURBULENCE

One beautiful fall morning in 1999, my friend Steve D. and I decided to fly from suburban Chicago to Fort Wayne, Indiana, to visit my parents. I taxied the red and blue Cessna 172 onto the runway and climbed away from runway two-six uneventfully. As we settled into our cruising altitude, Steve noticed that I scanned one particular instrument on the panel more often than the others. "What's that gauge with the miniature airplane in it?" he asked.

"That's the attitude indicator," I replied.

"What do you mean, attitude indicator? How does a plane have an attitude?"

"The attitude of the plane is what we call the position of the aircraft in relation to the horizon. When an airplane climbs, it has a nose-high attitude, and the miniature plane on the attitude indicator has its nose above the horizon line."

Steve chimed in, "I get it. So when the plane is diving, it's in a nose-down attitude."

"You got it, my man!" I exclaimed. "The attitude indicator is the most important instrument, because it indicates the plane's positional status and its performance."

A pilot's attitude indicator is a major source of protection, quickly signaling if the plane is in trouble. If pilots keep the proper aircraft attitude, they're rarely in harm's way. But if the plane's attitude is unsafe—diving, wings stalling, graveyard spiraling, or completely inverted—the pilot faces grave danger, and completion of the flight is in jeopardy.

The attitude of a salesperson is just as critical to his or her safety. Sales superstars know that their attitude is the single greatest contributor to their level of resiliency. The right attitude helps top producers bounce back from both major setbacks and the day-to-day challenges of selling such as rejections, objections, and lost sales. It gets them back in the game, back on the horse, and back on course. The best attitude for salespeople blends *optimism, faith, courage, discipline, a commitment to maintaining health, a sense of humor,* and *a willingness to accept help from colleagues.*

Optimism

Optimism is the fundamental conviction that somehow, sooner or later, things will work out and you will reach sales success. It's the belief that the adversity you face in selling, and in life, is merely a temporary setback with a hidden potential benefit, if only you can uncover it. Sales masters have learned to make optimistic thinking the cornerstone of their daily attitude. It helps them roll with whatever punches their day throws them. They know that optimism is not a Pollyanna mindset or wishful thinking. They just choose to believe that troubling circumstances, bad situations, and negative events can all be overcome. They choose to perceive defeat as a challenge that simply requires a different strategy. Optimistic salespeople also bounce back more quickly after being dealt an upset. Less resilient salespeople tuck their tail between their legs and run home to watch another episode of *Jerry Springer* or *Ricki Lake* and wallow in knowing that it could be worse.

When we change our thoughts, we change our world.
—NORMAN VINCENT PEALE

An optimistic attitude bears directly on sales success—it's not just empty rhetoric. In the early 1980s, Metropolitan Life Insurance realized that they hired many salespeople who ultimately failed, despite possessing both aptitude/intelligence and high motivation to succeed. They hired Martin E.P. Seligman, Ph.D., former president of the American Psychological Association and author of *Learned Optimism,* to improve their hiring practices. Seligman found that a third characteristic of salespeople—optimism—was also critical for success. Top-scoring optimists outsold pessimists by 57 percent, and generally optimistic salespeople outsold their pessimistic counterparts by 31 percent. Salespeople can have inherent talent and a passionate desire to succeed, but if they can't handle rejection, objections, disappointments, lost sales, and some failure, they'll give up too soon.

Dr. Seligman's lifelong work in this area investigated how people respond to negative events, especially in terms of what they say to themselves to explain why those events happen. Seligman defined this self-talk as your *self-explanatory style.* For example, is your first thought when you lose a sale, "I'm just no good at this?" Or is it more like, "That buyer just couldn't see the benefits that my product brings?" Negative events are a given in sales, and an optimistic explanatory style helps you overcome the setback instead of being immobilized.

Seligman's research shows that when people have a pessimistic explanatory style, they often ruminate over and over about a failure until they develop what's known as *learned helplessness.* They believe that they can do nothing to turn a setback into a comeback. Learned helplessness is the antithesis of resilience and the precursor to depression. The good news, however, is that Seligman also discovered that we can learn to become more optimistic. For salespeople, this translates into two key actions: supercharging your psychology and disputing pessimistic thoughts.

Supercharging your psychology. In Chapter 2, we learned that supercharging your psychology was an important part of entering your supercharged selling state. It's also clear that optimism is related to your peak state. A pessimistic attitude can drive salespeople into such a negative state that selling becomes arduous and even painful.

The same methods for supercharging your psychology and controlling your mental focus also help build an optimistic attitude. For example, building your C-CORE and developing beliefs that sales problems are not pervasive or permanent lead to an optimistic explanatory style. A strong sense of purpose and inspiring goals help you experience setbacks as "light turbulence" instead of "heavy chop." In addition, visualization, incantation, and asking better questions help direct your thoughts after negative events and can build an affirming explanatory style.

An example illustrates how salespeople can use their explanatory style to build optimism and stay in their peak state for selling. Our two sample insurance salespeople, Joe Pessimism and Jane Optimism, start with a list of potential buyers (identified ideal buyers) to call. They both begin the engagement process by telephone cold calling, which as mentioned earlier, is the number-one dreaded sales activity of all time. Most potential insurance buyers respond with, "No, I'm not interested," or, worse, just hang up.

After several negative calls, Joe says things to himself like, "I'm no good at cold calling," or "No one wants to buy these types of policies anymore." Or he might say, "I'm not even getting up to bat with this list of prospects." This kind of self-talk drives Joe into a negative state, which causes him to give up and makes it much harder to call the next prospective buyer. After a few of these episodes, Joe will be in such an unresourceful state that he'll call it a day. And after a few weeks, months, or years, Joe either gives up altogether or accepts marginal sales results and a marginal paycheck.

Jane, on the other hand, talks to herself in far more constructive ways after those initial negative calls. "He must be really busy right now," or "Let me tweak my phone script a little bit. I'm getting very close to having a script that really works." Or she might say, "Because every single no gets me closer to a yes, I'm getting very close to a sale." If Jane is a top pro, she might even say something bold like, "Let me hug that no, because more nos eventually lead to more yeses." This kind of self-talk helps Jane stay in a supercharged selling state, which makes that next call easier to dial and keeps her going until she connects and makes an appointment. The appointment energizes Jane and builds even more optimism, so she's eager to keep dialing for still another appointment.

Jane and Joe show us that you can build optimistic attitudes by how you talk to yourself and explain the obstacles inherent in selling, and that optimism keeps you in your supercharged selling state longer.

Disputing pessimistic thoughts. The method that Dr. Seligman developed for building optimism consists of recognizing and disputing pessimistic thoughts. He observed that we often make negative statements to ourselves (internal self-talk) about what we can or can't accomplish. We then fail to argue with those statements, even when we might have done so if another person had made the same comments. The key to increasing optimism, therefore, is to catch yourself being negative, ask yourself questions that will dispute your negative thoughts, and then use enabling self-talk to direct your mind more positively.

In our peak performance and sales success seminars, we use a modified version of Dr. Seligman's model that combines disputing pessimistic responses with asking yourself better questions to redirect your thoughts toward greater optimism. It follows an ABCD acronym.

- A *stands for Adversity.* You must identify any negative situation with which you deal.
- B *stands for Beliefs.* The thoughts you have in reaction to a negative event (cold calling or rejection, for example) usually congeal into beliefs when that situation occurs regularly.
- C *stands for Catch yourself.* The crux of becoming more optimistic is to catch yourself falling into a negative pattern of thoughts (beliefs) in reaction to an event, particularly with those that are habitual. After an adverse event, conduct a self-inventory of your response and your state.
- D *stands for Dispute and re-Direct.* Once you discover that you're running negative thoughts in your mind, you must dispute the evidence and/or redirect your thoughts by asking yourself better questions. By effectively disputing your beliefs and redirecting the thoughts that follow a negative event, you can change your reaction from dejection and giving up to activity and success.

It's essential to remember that your beliefs are just beliefs—they may or may not be based on facts. You want to dispute any negative beliefs that you routinely experience after a sales setback. If a belief is based on fact, then you must reframe the fact to put it in a more positive light. Here's an example.

- *Adversity.* I lost a big sale to the competitor today.
- *Beliefs and thoughts.* I always lose the big sales. My sales are at 34 percent of quota through the first six months of this year, and last year I was at only 88 percent of quota. Losing this sale means I will never be able to hit quota this year. I'm not ever going to be able to turn my sales career around.
- *Catch yourself.* Wow, am I having negative thoughts, or *what?* I'm in a very negative state and feel like crap. This is the point when that book, *Power Selling,* said I must catch myself.
- *Dispute and re-Direct.* Maybe I'm overreacting a bit. I don't *always* lose the big sales, do I? Didn't I close one at XYZ Hospital six weeks ago that was even bigger than the one I lost today? I could still hit my quota for year-end if I can put six more system sales opportunities into the funnel and close three that are in the funnel right now. What else can I do to turn this around? It's still *possible* that I can turn my territory around and become the sales champion I deserve to be. I want to make that Glamour Trip to Hawaii, too. I'm going to lay out a new, stronger marketing and telephone engagement plan to fill my funnel. Let's go!

Disputing negative beliefs and redirecting your thoughts elevate your optimism. The more you practice catching your negative beliefs, disputing them vigorously and aiming them more positively, the more optimistic your attitude will become, and the more resiliency you will develop.

Last night, after I finished writing, the Chicago Cubs's hopes of ending a 58-year drought without a World Series were dealt a deathblow by the Florida Marlins. The Marlins came from behind to win 9-6 in Game 7 of the National League Championship series. Pessimists say the Cubs were cursed by the "Billy Goat." How could they blow a 3-1 lead? Optimists say that this was one of the best years the Cubs have ever had. They won 96 games and lost 66, as compared to the year before, when they won 67 games but lost 95. Dusty Baker's leadership was great, the lineup for the next season (including pitching) is awesome, and it's always *possible* to win the World Series next year. For the Chicago Cubs to win the World Series, though, they may require some supernatural optimism. They may require faith!

Faith

Building the best attitude for resiliency also requires a certain amount of faith. Great pilots who have flown through harrowing situations during war often comment afterward that they have no idea *how* they made it. They know that their own abilities alone never could have carried them through to safety. They believe that God guided them and did what they couldn't.

Elite sales stars who make the long flight and who endure a long and rewarding career often share that same faith. Selling professionals who have achieved career success, financial prosperity, and fulfillment in all aspects of their lives, including family and friends, and who are genuinely happy have faith in a power greater than themselves. They know that their success is beyond what their own skills alone could produce. Life is far more rich and complex than what the physical eye can comprehend, and the greatest things to believe in can never be seen unless we choose to believe in them.

> *Faith is to believe in what we do not see;*
> *and the reward of this faith is to see what we believe.*
> **—ST. AUGUSTINE**

Resilience is needed for the trials and tribulations of life. Relational, financial, or health hardships strike everyone at one time or another. In those dark hours, when every fiber of your being is tested, believing in something greater than yourself opens you up to solutions and possibilities you never dreamed were possible. Such faith gives you the conviction that a way will be found, and it shapes your attitude to remain hopeful. I am here to be a witness that nothing can make you more resilient than trusting in God, because I have experienced this in my own life. Knowing that God will see me through whatever trials come my way keeps me in the game when I might otherwise quit.

Courage and Discipline

A resilient attitude also depends on courage and discipline. You might think of courage in connection with dramatic events, like surviving a plane being shot down behind enemy lines or running into the World Trade Towers on 9/11 to save a life. But everyday courage matters, too. It takes courage to get back up from the mat after losing a big sale. It takes courage to keep making those calls when the rejections pile up. It takes courage not to give up when your sales numbers appear bleak. John Abdo and Rudy Garcia-Tolson both demonstrated tremendous courage when they turned their setbacks into comebacks.

> *Courage is not the absence of fear; it's deciding ahead of time*
> *that something else is more important.*
> **—MIA'S FATHER, IN *THE PRINCESS DIARIES***

Sales superstars act with courage in those moments of choice between a negative event and their response. They have disciplined themselves to regulate their actions by principle, purpose, and judgment rather than by impulse, immediate gratification, or peer pressure. The selling elite have the discipline to do what is necessary, *when* it is necessary, whether they feel like it or not.

In a great essay by E. M. Gray titled "The Common Denominator of Success," he contends that one common denominator of all successful people is not hard work, good luck, or great communications skills, though those are all important. The one habit that transcends all others is discipline. Successful salespeople do what the average salespeople don't like to do. They probably don't *like* to do these tasks, either, but their purpose and goals drive them on. They exercise the muscle called discipline.

Gary Player, one of golf's greatest athletes, is a great role model for the discipline necessary to build resilience and achieve sales success. Once, when being interviewed, Player said, "Throughout my career, people have said to me, 'I'd give anything to hit a golf ball like you.'" Gary, who has always been known for being polite and dignified, said that on one particularly tough day, his politeness failed him when a spectator repeated that statement. Gary said he lost his cool and responded, "No you wouldn't! You would love to hit a golf ball like me *if it was easy!* Do you know what you have to go through to hit a golf ball the way I do? You've got to get up every morning at five o'clock, go out to the range, and hit 1,000 balls. Your hands start bleeding; then you walk back to the clubhouse, wash the blood off, slap on bandages, and then go out and hit another 1,000 balls. That's what it takes to hit a golf ball the way I do." Gary Player was resilient enough to endure such hardship day after day, because his courage and discipline formed an attitude that would not quit.

Other Factors

Several other factors help create a resilient attitude. Supercharging your physiology, keeping your sense of humor, and accepting help from others all help turn setbacks into comebacks.

Remember from Chapter 2 that one of the fastest ways to change how you feel, think, and act is to use your body differently? By changing your physiology, you change your state, and by changing your state, you change how you feel. Improving how you feel better equips you to handle negative situations and events. You can bounce back from failed situations much faster. Exercise, meditation, and music all work to improve your state and build resiliency. A good energy reserve also keeps you healthy and gives you the stamina to weather greater adversity and fight back.

Distracting yourself from your problems is also a viable tactic for regaining optimism—it's okay to take short breaks from your troubles. Remember Lillian N. from Chapter 1? She was often able to work past problems by *power shopping* for a few hours! Whether you run or shop, distracting yourself can leave you refreshed and ready to go again.

Humor, which we discussed in Chapter 4 as a great rapport builder, also shapes a resilient attitude. It helps you gain perspective during challenging times and relieves the tension that can kill resiliency. Humor keeps you fluid and flexible in difficult times. Recall that humor also produces a series of physiological reactions that improve both health and resiliency. If Norman Cousins, author of *Anatomy of an Illness*, can heal his way back from cancer to health by using laughter, then a stressed-out or negative salesperson can surely improve his or her attitude with it. Great sales masters all have the ability to laugh at themselves and their troubles.

Every pilot knows that calling for help on the radio during emergencies is the right thing to do. They know that air traffic control and other pilots are always ready to guide them to safety. Average salespeople forget this, but the superstars don't.

Most salespeople have a tendency to attempt to overcome all adversity on their own. While the rugged "pull yourself up by the bootstraps" approach can perhaps be admirable, salespeople usually do better when they seek each other's input and empathy. Knowing that you're not all alone in your struggles boosts your resiliency and willingness to come at it again. We reach out for help, not because we're weak but because we want to remain strong.

Ace flyers rely on their attitude indicator to keep their plane safe and flying on course. The plane's attitude directs them around or through emergencies to reach their destination. Sales superstars are no different. Their attitude relies on optimism, faith, courage, discipline, health, humor, and their support group to give them the resiliency that can handle sales turbulence. Here are your Power Boosters to build the attitude for sales success.

POWER BOOSTERS

- Read Dr. Seligman's book, *Learned Optimism,* and determine your own optimism quotient.

- Identify three negative sales situations you've been involved with in the last 14 days and practice the ABCD technique for turning your thinking around.

- Identify one or two sales situations (cold calling, group presentations, closing, etc.) where you habitually respond pessimistically, and practice the ABCD technique.

- Be a spiritual seeker (if you're not already) and explore your own beliefs about faith in a higher power.

- Practice using your discipline and courage in moments of choice where you must be resilient.

- Identify a support group that can help you bounce back when the challenges seem too great.

- Have a laugh! Go see a funny movie or tell a few jokes when the going gets tough.

- Exercise religiously and maintain good health.

IT'S NOT OVER UNTIL YOU WIN—
REACHING YOUR DESTINATION

Ace flyers recognize that their flight is not over until they make it to their destination and hear the screech of tires safely on the runway. We've already seen that unexpected events like turbulence or in-flight emergencies require pilots to be alert and flexible. Good pilots also know that the key points of any flight, such as takeoffs and landings, present significant challenges and demand increased workload. They identify those points in advance and prepare accordingly so they're at their very best. They know it's not over until they arrive.

When I learned to fly, landings scared me stiff. Trying to put that plane down on a 50-foot wide runway at 65 knots (75 mph) was like trying to thread a needle while riding a bucking bronco. I constantly had to adjust the attitude of the plane (power and pitch) while I tried to line it up perfectly with the runway. At the same time, I had to deal with gusty crosswinds, talk frequently on the radio, watch for converging traffic, and continually monitor my descent angle and rate. Coming in low or slow would put quite a damper on my evening plans. One time, I actually ran the plane off the runway and into the grass! But, through training, I became determined to land the plane safely no matter what. I was determined to arrive at my destination.

Top sellers also recognize that their journey is not over until they arrive at their destination—sales stardom! Just like pilots, they identify the key points in their journey where they will encounter the greatest challenges. Sales slumps, fear of rejection, call rejection, and buyer objections can occur both daily or occasionally during a sales career. Preparing for these demands opens your resiliency throttle full tilt to arrive on the red-carpeted airstrip of sales success. *Turning fear into power, soaring out of a sales slump,* and *repelling the objections* are three types of situations where sales superstars know they must be determined to work through adversity to arrive at success.

Turning Fear into Power

Fears can cripple a salesperson's resiliency. They are one component of the selling journey where challenges are great and thorough training is needed. Call reluctance, avoidance, procrastination, doubt, and anxiety all stem from fear and infect most salespeople. These behavioral symptoms of fear can prevent them from reaching peak earnings, recognition, and superstar status. If you're reading this and thinking this is not you *all* the time, it probably *is* you some of the time. We all catch the call reluctance "bug" from time to time.

Why would salespeople begin their day, shower and dress, and have the very best intentions of making a lot of quality calls but then waste the day by doing everything *but* make the calls? Fear of rejection is usually the reason.

Fear of rejection reflects your sense of self and the ability of your ego to handle the word *no*. If you're afraid of being rejected, you'll begin to protect yourself by avoiding sales situations where you perceive rejection is likely. The problem with this plan is that by doing so, you also end up avoiding those situations where a sale is possible.

The truth about all fears is that they never go away as long as you're committed to growing and stepping out of your comfort zone. But if you knew that you could handle any sales rejection that came your way, what would you possibly fear? NOTHING! All you have to do to diminish your fear is to develop more trust in your ability to handle whatever comes your way. The way to desensitize yourself and overcome the fear of cold calling or sales rejection is to simply go out and *do that which you fear.* Ultimately, pushing through the fear is less frightening than living with the underlying, vague anxiety that comes from self-protective strategies. Working to resolve your fears actually increases your adaptability and resiliency, and it gets you closer to your destination.

> *We should not let our fears hold us back from pursuing our hopes.*
> **—JOHN F. KENNEDY**

There are several steps to break through any sales-related fear. First, work constantly to build up your C-CORE (competence, confidence, commitment, and character), which you need to navigate through fear.

Second, practice entering the *supercharged selling state* (Chapter 2) every day, so you'll have the passion that blasts past fear. Identify the particular fear that's holding you back, create a movie (visualization) of your breaking through, and run that movie every day until you're not immobilized. Do the same with incantation and asking yourself better questions. Get your daily prime-time in. Use the ABCD technique (from this chapter) if you find that you're rationalizing about not approaching a potential buyer, difficult client, or challenging situation.

Third, use whatever strategy is appropriate to stack the deck in your favor. The more precall research (family history) you've conducted, the greater your confidence will be. Arming yourself with a powerful tool, like a great telephone script, will also greatly reduce your fear level. Fear is nothing but a wake-up call to be more prepared.

Fourth, and most importantly, *decide* to break through your fear and not be immobilized by it ever again. Believe that you can triumph over fear, and turn fear into power.

What's the difference between the sales rep who's making $65,000 a year and the one who's making $265,000 a year? The superstars don't let rejection stop them from putting it all on the line. Remember that, although the great Babe Ruth scored more home runs than anyone else in his era, he also had the most strike-outs. The selling elite are the ones who are rejected the most in the majority of industries, but they take *no* as just a little prod to keep going until they hear *yes*. They have fallen in love with *no*, just like these people:

- Sylvester Stallone was rejected more than 1,000 times when he first started out. He kept hugging those *nos* and finally ended up making a movie called *Rocky*. He was able to hear *no* 1,000 times and then still knock on door 1,001.
- Louis L'Amour, the author of more than 100 western novels that have sold 200 million copies, received over 350 rejections before he made his first sale.
- Colonel Sanders, at the age of 65, was put out of business by a road construction project. He also got rejected more than 1,000 times trying to sell his chicken recipe with 11 herbs and spices. Finally, at age 75, the Colonel sold his fried chicken company for a finger lickin' $15 million.

There are no real successes without rejection. The more rejection you get, the more you've learned, the greater your resiliency, and the closer you are to your success destination. The bottom line is this: If you fall in love with *no*, then you've beaten the fear of rejection and turned fear into power.

Soaring out of a Sales Slump

A slump is another place on your sales journey where you can lose your way and never reach the top of your career. The truth is that no one can sustain peak performance day in and day out, 200 days per year. Everybody has off days, but a bona fide slump comes when those days string themselves into weeks or months. You're doing the things that made you successful before, but now they don't work. You begin to question your competence, doubt your confidence, and wonder if you're a sales wiener instead of a sales winner. Your self-esteem shrinks to the size of a walnut, fear kicks in before every call, and you wonder how to break the cycle of doom.

It may comfort you to know that every sales master has had a slump at one time or another. The problem is really never the slump but how we respond to it. My dad taught me one way to kick a slump when I was just a kid learning to play golf. He told me to have a very short memory. When I would slice the ball, top the ball, or even miss the ball, he told me to forget it and get psyched up for the next shot. Don't fret over mistakes you've already made—look ahead to the next step. This outlook keeps you moving toward your goals and able to bounce back from a slump.

When salespeople go into a slump, they avoid filling their sales funnel, they procrastinate on follow-up, and they generally stop doing the activities that could increase sales and end the slump. The Catch-22 is that the typical response to a sales slump just makes it worse.

It is hard to beat a man who never gives up.
—BABE RUTH

Knowing that slumps will occur and devising a plan ahead of time for coming out of one increase your bounce-back ability. The first step is to acknowledge the slump and then take a day off! Go to a movie, start a novel, see a ball game, or just take a nap in an outdoor hammock (hopefully in a warm climate). This step may seem paradoxical, because you're not actually *doing* sales activities, but it's important to relax and cleanse your mind of stress and frustration.

The second step is to remember a time in your past when you've been resilient. Recall when you overcame disappointment in your selling career, beat out a competitor, or secured a big sale that had appeared lost. Or recall a time from your personal life when you came back from a disappointment. Maybe somebody told you that you had no talent in an area or that you could not accomplish a particular goal, and you later proved them wrong. I remember completing the 1998 Disney Marathon or completing my flight training—these memories help me turn it around whenever I find myself in a slump.

The third step is to get back in the habit of your daily prime time and make sure you enter every day in a supercharged selling state. Affirm that you have the ability to bounce back. Decide that you are going to be like the Timex watch that takes a licking and keeps on ticking.

The fourth step is to put together a new strategic business plan. Go back to identifying your ideal buyers and redo your target account list. Include a sales funnel assessment and identify your hot ones, decide how many new leads you need to add to the sales funnel, and list what steps must be taken to nurture those that are in the funnel. Consult with your colleagues or management until you feel damn good about your new game plan. Then plan out an initial ten-day blitz deploying a high-energy assault to start turning things around. Take your new battle plan and hit the ground running. Be like the Energizer Bunny that just keeps going and going and going.

These steps will get you through the challenges of a sales slump and keep you moving toward your sales success destination. They'll build the resiliency you need to turn a slump setback into a comeback.

Repelling the Objections

Another place in the journey to sales stardom where salespeople are likely to encounter significant challenges is when they deal with buyer objections. These perceived setbacks send average salespeople into a panic, but sales superstars have prepared in advance for overcoming them and don't let them deter the sales process. Voicing an objection is one way that buyers protect themselves from salespeople and keep them at bay. Buyers usually fear change, so they'll object about price or a feature, even if just out of habit. "That price seems high," or, "We don't really need the faxing capability, too," or maybe, "Isn't it a hassle to operate this?" Buyers use these objections to hold salespeople off and control them.

Average salespeople let objections cumulatively wear down their resilience, while the pros just smile inwardly. The superstars know three secrets about buyer objections. First, they don't *handle* objections, as most sales training teaches—instead, they *repel* them. Top producers *prevent* objections in the first place by following the strategies you've already learned in this book. Second, they know that objections are merely warning signals to go back and retrace their steps using RPM Questioning. Third, they know that late objections that were not repelled can easily be overcome.

> *The man who really wants to do something finds a way;*
> *the other man finds an excuse.*
> **—E. C. MCKENZIE**

Average salespeople prescribe too much without a thorough diagnosis and present too many or the wrong features (those not tied to the benefits the buyer said were important). They end up fueling the buyer's objections. If you present unrelated benefits or are unprofessional in the manner in which you present your solution, you increase buyers' concerns about your capability to deliver what they need. All objections are the result of a poor selling process, which ultimately leads to a lack of trust. But if you master identification, diagnosis, and prescription, you'll eliminate most objections.

Objections early in the selling process, before buyers have a vision of your solution, usually indicate that they want and need space. This happens when you start throwing features or advantages (prescribing before uncovering the benefits that are relevant to the buyer) at the buyer too soon. These objections are a sign to go back and use the R and P questions to finish your diagnosis. Then, after confirming your diagnosis, you can present the benefits and related features that are important to the buyer. This strategy repels objections that occur early in the selling process.

Most salespeople panic when they get objections late in the selling process, after the buyer appeared to agree with their diagnosis and prescription for the solution. Why? Because it seems as if the buyer has changed their mind "overnight." The top selling professional, on the other hand, views the late-stage objection positively, because it's a *value objection*. Value objections are objections about risk and indicate that the buyer has agreed with your solution but needs a nudge to get past the fear of making the wrong decision or paying too much.

Value objections can be overcome by asking more M questions to magnify the pain of not purchasing and the gain of purchasing. Any remaining value objections that surface can be dealt with by making benefit statements and sharing reference success stories that show how your product's value exceeds their risk. You must remind buyers of their pain, their vision of the solution, and the proof that the value exceeds the risk. Empathize with them and let them vent. Very often, buyers who object at the end stages simply want you to validate their discomfort and have you reassure them that they're making a good decision. Agree with the buyers that they're making a big decision. Comfort them and let them know that you're partners in a longer-term relationship. If they see you panic at their objections, their own fear of making a bad decision can escalate to the point where the sale is lost.

Fears, sales slumps, and buyer objections are all key phases in the sales journey where top producers must depend on their resiliency to get them through. Superstars refuse to let any of these setbacks interfere with their resolve to reach their destination of sales success. They know that it's not over until they've made it to stardom! These Power Boosters will keep you on your journey to success.

POWER BOOSTERS

- Commit to break through any fear that immobilizes you (even if it hampers you only occasionally).

- Get some prime time and step into your supercharged selling state every day.

- Use the telephone and face-to-face engagement rules, along with a great script, to reduce cold calling fear.

- Develop a short memory for previous sales blunders, screw-ups, and poor results.

- Recall a time or two when you've bounced back from failure and play those movies to blast past fear and soar out of a slump.

- Repel objections by using RPM questioning, and don't overpresent features.

- Don't panic when you hear an objection—just smile, make benefit statements, and share reference stories so that the value outweighs the risk.

- Comfort buyers and reassure them that they're making a good decision when you receive late-stage value objections.

LET'S RECAP

Sales superstars turn every setback into a comeback in their flight to victory. They accept adversity as part of the selling life, and they take personal responsibility for overcoming any and all challenges. They rely on optimism, faith, courage, and discipline to build an attitude that keeps them in the game. They never give up until they've reached success. Sales masters are committed to turn fear into power, soar out of any sales slumps, and repel buyer objections to reach their destination.

If we were to get out our trusty electron microscope again to look at the DNA of a man named Bill Porter, we would find the genetic fibers *reputation, real passion, research, rapport,* and *resource management* occupying the first five strands. On the sixth strand, we would see a pronounced enlargement of fibers. Mr. Porter's sixth strand, *resiliency,* is a genetic wonder.

Bill Porter was born in 1932, and the delivery was tough—brain damage resulted in cerebral palsy. But, despite a lifelong disability and the constant slamming of doors, Bill became more than a sales superstar; he became a *sales hero.* Bill, a door-to-door salesperson, is one of the most resilient salespeople the world has ever known. Once during an ice storm, he crawled the last part of his seven-mile route on his hands and knees. He describes that day—which included dragging his briefcase full of catalogs and samples up an icy driveway—as "one of the best selling days I ever had! Many people were home because of the storm; it was great!"

Bill Porter's routine for more than 38 years has been the same. He gets up at 4:45 each morning and spends 90 minutes dressing himself before he catches a 7:30 bus, which takes him to his Portland, Oregon, territory to start by 9:00. He then returns home after a 14-hour day, exhausted and aching, and retires for the night. Every two weeks, he types up his orders with one finger, which takes him more than ten hours, so that someone can deliver all the spices, foods, and home health remedies his clients have purchased.

Nothing dampens his enthusiasm. If someone refuses to open a door or slams one in his face, he silently repeats the mantra, "The next customer will say yes." Although the Watkins Company now has more than 60,000 salespeople, Bill is the only one still selling door-to-door. Most people now buy the company's products through discount stores and catalogs. But Bill never complains or makes excuses. He simply keeps on keeping on—getting into his territory each day and taking care of his loyal clients.

Despite millions of slammed doors, and after working more than 24 years for the Watkins Company, Bill Porter finally reached his dream. Bill Porter became the top salesperson in the Watkins Company's western division and became the first recipient of the prestigious Chairman's Award for Dedication and Commitment. He turned every setback he ever encountered into a dramatic comeback.

THE POWER OF RELATIONSHIPS

Convert Clients into Collaborative Partners

The salesperson who adds value after the sale clearly demonstrates that the relationship is more important than revenue, and the person is more important than profits.
—TODD DUNCAN

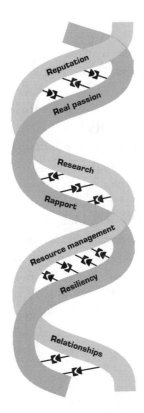

One cold Friday night in January 1991, the phone rang. "Is This Tom O.?" the caller asked.

"Yes, it is," Tom replied. "Who's this?"

"I'm Dr. Gary B. from XYZ Children's Hospital. I'm the new ortho surgeon here, and we have an emergency spinal case tomorrow. My technician and I don't know how to run the Cell Saver®, and neither does anybody else available to us. We have a six-year-old boy who really needs surgery now—he can't wait till Monday. Can you help run the device and train us, too? I used another brand back in Boston, and I can't reach that sales rep."

"I'll do it. What time do you need me?" Tom answered.

Dr. B. said, "Be here at 6:30 AM to scrub in."

The next morning, Tom ran the Cell Saver, which collects blood shed during surgery, separates the oxygen-carrying red cells, and returns them to the patient during the procedure. All went well in this four-hour operation. Dr. B. and his nursing team thanked Tom profusely for coming in on a Saturday, with such short notice, and going the extra mile for their patient.

About a year later, Tom received a phone call from the ABC Teaching Hospital in Minneapolis. The company he sold for had been completely locked out from getting any of the Cell Saver business at this hospital, but the purchasing agent on the phone wanted to fax a purchase order for seven Cell Savers, worth more than $100,000 in business. Tom was stunned and elated! He was also confused, because he hadn't even visited the hospital in over six months. The purchasing agent told him that their new chief of surgery, Dr. Gary B., refused to use any other type of equipment. Their order needed to be completed ASAP, and Tom ended up with a killer commission check.

By wowing Dr. Gary B. with incredible service, Tom O. used the Power of Relationships to create a loyal client who returned for more business. If we take a final peek under our special microscope, we see that the seventh genetic strand on a sales superstar's DNA is occupied by the Power of Relationships.

The ultimate goal of all selling activity is—sales! The most efficient way to generate those sales is to have customers who know and like you come back for repeat business. This leverages your efforts, because your reputation is already established, your research is already done, and you've already formed a solid base of rapport. The only way to develop this kind of client loyalty is through the Power of Relationships.

The sales elite excel in building relationships with their customers. They're driven by something bigger than money or recognition or prizes—they know it's all about the people. They have a burning desire to provide value to those clients whom they have the privilege to serve. As Zig Ziglar always says, "You can get everything in life you want, if you will just help enough other people get what they want." The focus on serving discussed in Chapter 1 does more than build a reputation; over the long haul, it matures into a trusting and collaborative partnership. Top producers move from simple rapport to collaborating with clients by creating mutually satisfying, long-term relationships. They become insiders in their buyers' organizations, which enables them to help their buyers with *their* clients and problems and gives them a great competitive advantage.

> *Offer your customers a long-term relationship,*
> *then do everything to build and maintain it.*
> **—BRIAN TRACY**

At 233 South Wacker Drive in Chicago stands an architectural superstar—the Sears Tower. It stands tall, far above the rest. An American role model, it's a triumph of ingenuity and innovation, reflecting strength, vision, and architectural excellence. It's North America's tallest building, towering 1,454 feet and 110 stories in the air. It has 35 miles of unparalleled views, and on clear days you can gaze at four states from the observation deck. The Tower has a remarkable 4.5 million square feet and was built with one of the most innovative structural support systems ever erected. Completed in 1974, at a cost of $150 million, the Sears Tower is an icon of engineering success.

Chicago, the Windy City, is known for giving headaches to high-rise architects, because the average wind speed is 16 miles per hour with gusts of 50 miles per hour or more. The Sears Tower's estimated weight—more than 440 million pounds—also presented a major engineering challenge. To build a skyscraper of that height and weight in Chicago conditions required a foundation that was magnificently strong and flexible. Nine structural tubes (75 feet wide) were connected to 114 rock caisson piles driven into the bedrock by 203 drilled shafts. The resulting foundation supported a skyscraper that's the world's largest in terms of square feet. The Sears Tower is recognized around the world as a *skyscraper superstar.*

The first step in building the Sears Tower was to commit to doing so. Bruce Graham and his architectural firm possessed a vision of what the finished product should look like, and they committed to designing whatever kind of foundation such a landmark skyscraper needed. They discovered that its foundation had to be deep—110 feet down into the rock—and wide. Without such a foundation, the Sears Tower would never stand up to Chicago's gales.

The skyscraper of sales success requires a foundation, too—one built of relationships with your clients. You must follow the same steps that Bruce Graham did to develop relationships that lead to high-level trust and loyalty. Begin by obtaining commitment from the buyer to formalize your buyer-seller relationship, then return your own commitment to deliver exceptional products and customer service. Deepen relationships with your ideal buyers by wowing them with impeccable follow-up, diligent problem solving, and quick resolution of service foul-ups. Widen your foundation by personally marketing yourself to reach more potential clients, including all buying influences within an account (especially C-level decision makers), and expanding your base of supportive non-client relationships. In short, the foundation of your sales success depends on remembering to *start with commitment, deepen your relationships,* and *widen your relational foundation.*

START WITH COMMITMENT

Architects commit to designing whatever foundation is required for their vision of the completed structure. The foundation contractor must also sign a formal agreement and commit to work on the project before materials get delivered to the site and construction actually begins. A lack of commitment from either party will terminate the project, as one of my neighbors recently discovered when she attempted to hire a designer to redo her kitchen. He seemed interested, and she ordered new cabinets and tile, but he never showed up or called her back. His lack of commitment stopped the job dead.

Salespeople must also "design" their relationships with buyers and have a long-term vision of what a healthy relationship looks like. Top producers take steps to make that vision a reality, and they know it begins with commitment. First, they must obtain commitment from the buyer to purchase their product or service, if they want the relationship to move to the next level or eventually develop into collaboration. This step is commonly referred to as closing the sale, but in reality, it's *opening the relationship,* because the salesperson must reciprocally commit to serving the buyer long term. Second, sales stars commit to the principle of *relational banking.*

Closing the Sale—But Opening the Relationship

Commitment to the buyer-seller relationship occurs at many levels. Every single sales call you ever make requires obtaining commitment to advance the sales process, so every single sales call requires a closing. You may not be closing the sale itself—especially in larger, complex sales—but you must seek commitment from the buyer to take the next step. Fifty percent of all sales conversations end without the salesperson asking for a subsequent meeting or the order itself—but that's *not* how the superstars do it. Salespeople who fear asking the buyer for the business end up becoming just "professional visitors"—and if you're just a professional visitor, it won't be long before your creditors will come and take away your furniture! The selling elite seek commitment. They seek commitment because they want their relationship with the buyer eventually to be characterized by trust, loyalty, and collaboration, and this initial commitment propels the relationship to the next level. If they don't get it, the superstars try again and again. They have *polite persistence.* They seek commitment expectantly, courteously, and in a friendly manner, but they always keep seeking. They know that obtaining commitment should be viewed as *opening a relationship* instead of *closing a sale.* This relationship could lead to a loyal client and a repetitive sales stream. It's not a closing, but an opening; not an ending, but a beginning.

No other area of sales training receives as much attention as closing the sale. Assumptive closes, invitational closes, direct closes, alternative closes, order-blank closes, the Ben Franklin close, the puppy dog close, the banana close, the hot potato close, the sharp-angle close, the take-away close, the boomerang close, the double-whammy close, and the you're-a-moron-if-you-don't-take-this close are some of the most revered techniques. Neil Rackham's great research, however, discovered that closing techniques generally increase the chances of making a sale only with low-priced products—they actually reduce the chances of making a sale with expensive products or services.

The truth is that potential buyers will close their own sales if you offer them valuable solutions, which they can see will meet their needs. Great selling at the end of the sales cycle is about controlling the process, *not* the buyer. People love to buy but hate to be sold. When buyers are convinced that your solution relieves pain or provides gain, they will take action, because it feels good for them to buy. Sales masters who follow the strategies of *Power Selling* actually need to close less often, because their buyers will *offer* to buy.

Your sales process with a potential buyer will eventually reach the point where both of you know that the next logical step is a commitment to purchase. If you've been a keen observer through every phase of the sales process, you'll be able to sense when buyers are receptive. They will demonstrate buying signals that you can see or listen to. Positive body language—like leaning forward (remember Mitsy K. with the doctor in Chapter 4), smiling, nodding their heads, or becoming more animated—are all strong indicators. When potential buyers start asking questions about price, value, or deliverables or request additional proof sources or references, you know that they're close to buying, and you can lead them toward the commitment.

When buyers ask you questions at this stage, you should avoid answering with a yes or no response. If the buyer says, "Can you deliver by the end of November?" and you say no, you may lose the sale. If you respond with, "Do you need it by the end of November?" or, "Tell me more about why the timing is so critical," you're more likely to manage the potential buyer's expectations and secure the sale, whether you can meet the shipping deadline or not.

If you can think of any legitimate reason why the buyer cannot or will not buy today, then the buyer can think of it also. Last-minute value objections can be handled easily by using RPM Questioning and by sharing benefit statements and reference success stories, as we learned in Chapter 6. If you sense that the time is not right, be patient. Attempting to obtain commitment prematurely—closing before the deal is closeable—destroys the buyer's trust and can lose the sale. If you've behaved as a true Doctor of Selling, you will have already diagnosed your potential buyer's area of pain, confirmed your diagnosis, and prescribed a solution that the buyer saw as *the* solution. With these steps behind you, the time for commitment will be obvious to both you and your buyer. There are three steps to obtaining a commitment for purchase.

1. Confirm that all concerns have been addressed.
2. Restate your prescription's benefits.
3. Propose or ask for the commitment.

When the potential buyer doesn't ask you outright to purchase, there are three easy steps to follow to obtain commitment. First, simply ask if there are any further concerns that need to be addressed and then respond to them. Skipping this step can lead right into asking for commitment prematurely and losing the sale. Second, restate all the benefits that are part of your prescription. Make sure that every single benefit the buyer said was important is anchored to eliminating pain or delivering gain, again helping the buyer to associate a positive state with your solution. And third, ask buyers for their business—propose a commitment to purchase in whatever manner best fits your style and product.

Proposing a commitment may be as simple as saying, "I suggest we ship the CAT scanner to you next month and schedule training for the following month." You assume the close, and if they don't stop you, you've made the sale.

Asking for commitment may also mean asking potential buyers in a straightforward manner, with nonthreatening eye contact, if they're ready to proceed. It's generally more effective to refrain from using questions that could be answered with a no. "When do you want this delivered?" "Which warehouse should we ship this to?" "How much escrow do you want to put down?" "Which configuration do you want delivered?" These are examples of questions that obtain commitment. There are thousands more. They key is to find those that work best for you.

> *The only pressure that you use in selling is the presence of silence*
> *after the closing question.*
> **—BRIAN TRACY**

After you've asked for commitment, the oldest rule in selling still applies—*shut up!* Tension may rise, and a minute can seem like an hour, but you must be quiet and radiate unshakable confidence. Potential buyers who are on the fence will respond better to quiet strength than they will to more talking.

When a potential buyer becomes a buyer, take note of the transition together. Celebrate how good it feels to close business—congratulate your buyers on their wise decision and emphasize how it's a win-win for both of you. Enjoy your sale and their purchase!

Sales superstars also make this the time when they commit to the relationship and begin to develop high-level trust with their clients. When it comes to relationships, the difference between the rookie and the all-pro is how they treat their clients after the sale. Superstars commit to the relationship—they promise to serve to the best of their ability by taking all the steps necessary to retain the client for as long as possible. They know that the "hunter mentality" of one-shot, quick-fix transactions will prevent them from getting repeat business and eventually becoming a consultative partner. They don't commit to all buyers equally, because they remember the Pareto Principle that 20 percent of clients produce 80 percent of sales, but they make some level of conscious commitment to build a better relationship. Long-term relationships founded on trust that, through the consistent delivery of exceptional service, has matured to a high level produce the most lucrative results. In short, sales superstars commit to their clients after the sale and commit to long-term relationships with clients who prove to be worth the investment.

Commit to Relational Banking

The second step that sales masters follow in creating long-term relationships with buyers that match their vision of loyal partnerships is the principle of relational banking. Stephen Covey's great metaphor of the emotional bank account describes the way that trust can be built up with your clients.

Think about how a financial bank account works. You make deposits and build up a monetary reserve so that you can make withdrawals when needed. In relational banking, you build up an emotional reserve of trust with the client by staying committed, being honest, and focusing on service. The more of these deposits you make, the higher the trust and the greater the accumulated relational wealth.

When you waver in your commitment, break promises, and under-serve your client, you make withdrawals. The greater the number of withdrawals, the smaller the remaining reserve in your emotional bank account. Eventually, if you make too many withdrawals, your account will become overdrawn. At that point, the client opens an account with someone else. Unlike many personal relationships, buyers today have zero tolerance for overdrawn accounts, because they have so many other salespeople vying for their business. Nothing overdraws your relational account with clients faster than not following through on a promise that's important to them. Making too many withdrawals leads straight to relational bankruptcy.

We have committed the Golden Rule to memory; let us now commit it to life.
—EDWIN MARKHAM

A key to sound relational banking is to apologize immediately when you or your company makes a withdrawal. Your client is far more likely to remain loyal if they hear words like, "I'm sorry, I screwed up," or, "I'm sorry we didn't ship when we said we would. We were wrong." There will be times when you drop the ball. The selling elite take full and immediate responsibility, which shows respect for the client and maintains high-level trust.

Relational banking also means thanking your clients for their business. Thank them immediately, often, and creatively, so they know that you don't take their business for granted. A good example from Chapter 1 was sending out unique thank-you cards with million-dollar bills, but there are an infinite number of ways to say thank you.

Here are the Power Boosters to close the sale, open the relationship, and follow relational banking.

POWER BOOSTERS

- Always seek commitment. Develop polite persistence.

- Remember that obtaining commitment is about opening and not just closing.

(continued)

- Be a keen observer of both nonverbal and verbal cues at the end of the sales process.

- Avoid answering a potential buyer's question with a yes or no response.

- Memorize the three steps to obtaining commitment when the buyer doesn't outright offer to purchase.

  1. Confirm that all concerns have been addressed.

  2. Restate your prescription's benefits.

  3. Propose or ask for the commitment.

- Commit to client relationships after the sale and be prepared to deepen those relationships that fit your profile.

- Remember to make deposits and not withdrawals in the relational bank account with clients. Keep your commitments and follow through on your promises.

- Apologize whenever you or your company screws up.

- Thank your clients for their business!

DEEPEN YOUR RELATIONSHIPS

"She towers so high," were the words sung by a chorus of electrical contractors, as iron workers hoisted the final 2,500-pound girder into place to top off the Sears Tower. Who would have guessed that Richard Sears, who brought a fledgling mail-order business to Chicago in 1887, would get to have the world's tallest building (1973–1996) named after him? The city of Chicago and the rest of the world were awestruck by the black, shimmering structure that pierced the clouds and stood boldly above the other buildings.

While attention focused on the Tower's height, very few understood that this supreme tallness was possible only because of the depth of the foundation. The Sears Tower's foundation utilizes solid rock caissons drilled an amazing 110 feet deep into the bedrock of Mother Earth. As my dad used to always say, "She ain't goin' anywhere!"

The tower of sales success is much the same. The primary reason that top producers' sales numbers climb so high is the depth of the foundation they build. That foundation is formed by their relationships with clients. The selling elite reach bold, spectacular heights of sales success because they've deepened their client relationships to the point where they include loyalty and retention.

Deep seller-buyer relationships are mutually satisfying to both you and your clients—you're happy with the continued revenue stream, and they're pleased with the way you serve them. In general, those two factors—your financial gain and the buyer's satisfaction—vary together across a spectrum: the more satisfied your clients are, the more business you receive. Your clients' response to your relationship can range from satisfaction (the bare minimum level of service required to continue doing business with you) . . . to elation (your service exceeds their expectations) . . . to loyalty (your service has exceeded their expectations consistently and over time until they refuse even to consider the com-

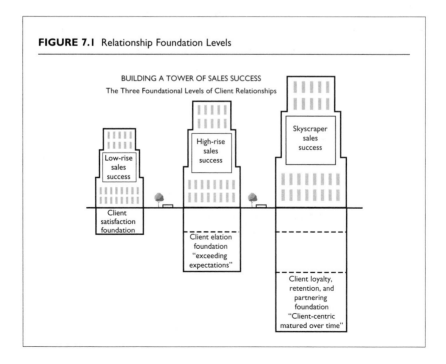

FIGURE 7.1 Relationship Foundation Levels

BUILDING A TOWER OF SALES SUCCESS
The Three Foundational Levels of Client Relationships

Low-rise sales success

High-rise sales success

Skyscraper sales success

Client satisfaction foundation

Client elation foundation "exceeding expectations"

Client loyalty, retention, and partnering foundation "Client-centric matured over time"

petition). Sales masters' buyers are at the loyalty end of the spectrum, and they welcome these pros as collaborative partners in their businesses.

How well do most salespeople do in generating client satisfaction? Not so hot—one in four buyers at any given time teeters on the brink of leaving for a competitor because of bad service. Of these, only one in 25 will ever tell you that they're dissatisfied—unless you ask them (so ask!). Jeffrey Gitomer, author of *The Sales Bible,* and Ty Boyd, customer service expert, report that only 5 percent of American businesses consistently exceed their clients' expectations.

I'm often frustrated at the passionless customer service that pervades American business today. I recently had trouble locating a certain model of shoes that I've purchased for nearly a decade at a Chicago shoe store. I asked a salesperson where the brand was, but she was unfamiliar with the shoes and doubted that I had purchased them there. How could this store run out of an item they had carried for ten years and not even be familiar with it? No one in the store offered to help me find it, direct me to someone who could find it, or even look it up. No one apologized for not having it or being unable to help a ten-year customer. I was neither satisfied nor elated, and loyalty was out the window, because I'll be shopping elsewhere from now on. Sales pros know that during their entire career, they'll always report to only one boss: the client. If you don't satisfy the client, the same thing always happens—you'll get fired!

In our sales seminars, we often ask how many salespeople can name their top 25 to 50 clients (the number depends on the industry) and what those clients' preferences are. Usually around 10 percent can, and these salespeople are driven by something bigger than money, recognition, or Glamour Trips. They're driven to serve their clients. *They love people.* They love to provide such great value and service that their clients routinely say, "Wow!"

> *If you could only love enough, you could be*
> *the most powerful person in the world.*
> **—EMMETT FOX**

These superstars are *client-centric.* They focus on serving at such a high level that their clients are wowed by how they do it. The difference between the rookie and the superstar is quite apparent—the rookie focuses on the product or the sale, while the pro focuses on the client.

Being client-centric means that you put your clients at the center of the universe.

Wowing your clients starts with service that's above and beyond the norm. Dropping the ball can lead to emotional bankruptcy, but superior service can build relationships and trust that leave your cash register clanging away. Top professionals know that the following methods for attending to their clients produce deep and rewarding relationships.

Join My Club

One way that sales masters provide outstanding service to their buyers and create higher levels of trust is to initiate them after the sale and welcome them into their own special club (see Chapter 1). Clients appreciate personalized service after the sale and the feeling that they're important to the salesperson.

Austin D., a medical monitoring salesperson, demonstrates this principle clearly. He always develops a customized clinical utilization booklet for every anesthesiologist on staff when a hospital purchases his equipment. The booklet is specifically tailored to the types of cases each doctor typically handles. Austin even creates a separate training booklet for all the nurses and technicians who assist in the monitoring. Hospital staffs rave about this level of after-sale assistance, because it makes their jobs easier, and it's something no other sales reps do. Austin's buyers are wowed!

Sally Z., a real estate superstar, also creates a special club when she gives every single property buyer (even those whom she didn't list) a customized notebook embossed with their names on it. The notebook is filled with everything a new property buyer could want such as relevant phone numbers (including her own); the contract; tax information; hand-sketched diagrams showing pertinent information about gas, water, and electrical switches; and an area map. Buyers don't usually expect such service, and they remember Sally when they want to buy again, even if she hadn't represented them previously. They hang on to these useful notebooks, and guess whose contact information is written all over it?

After-sale training and implementation of your product or service must include personally demonstrating your product's operation with all the end users in a way that goes beyond the skimpy five-minute overview that everyone has experienced from a poor automobile sales-person upon car delivery. Special treatment must recognize your buyers' uniqueness with personalized attention. The individualized gestures we discussed in Chapter 1—such as unique thank-you notes, birthday cards, congratulatory cards, and personal introductions of your support staff—make them feel like family. This is the essence of client-centric behavior, and it builds greater client loyalty.

Johnny "On-the-Spot"

Another method that sales superstars use to deepen relationships with buyers and achieve client loyalty and retention is to become Johnny "On-the-Spot." They develop impeccable follow-up, stay on top of the small details, anticipate what their clients need, and provide it before ever being asked to. Top producers know that they must respond to their client's needs quickly and dependably—before the client even has a chance to think about what another vendor might provide.

After spending more than ten years selling to cardiovascular sur-geons, I learned the importance of timely and responsive service. I could never tell a CV surgeon, "I'll try to get that oxygenator to you by Mon-day." When a patient is on the table for a quadruple bypass, if I couldn't deliver, the surgeon was livid. If any other vendor could supply the item, I was done—for good.

My only acceptable response was, "We'll have it there if I have to bor-row it from another hospital and drive it there myself." That's what the surgeon expects when a patient's life may be on the line. If all salespeople approached responsiveness with that sense of importance, they would lose far fewer clients.

Being Johnny "On-the-Spot" with follow-up also means having a sys-tem in place to find, reach, organize, and track clients. You must know who they are, what their preferences are, how to reach them easily, and when the next contact should take place.

I always find it amazing that few companies track client relationships by any system, despite the fact that those relationships are crucial for their success. Pharmaceutical companies don't track all the drugs their doc-tors dispense, real estate agents don't track buyer or seller preferences beyond the immediate transaction, and airlines rarely track whether a client prefers an aisle or window seat. Even clothing salespeople hardly ever track their clients' sizes and preferences. Even though there is so much buzz today about customer relationship management (CRM) systems, most companies just don't integrate their IT function to focus on the client and have a customized sales process to serve those clients. Most companies layer clients into their IT systems after all the product information is in place. As we say back in Indiana, that's back asswards.

You want to have a computer system in place that allows you to see clients' complete buying histories instantly. Another screen should have their birthdays, hobbies, children's names, and all the other information you gleaned from the Eight-Point Buyer Checklist (Chapter 3). This information is worth its weight in gold—it creates client elation and increases your market share of their business.

Even if your company doesn't get this, *you* should. Sales superstars know that the more information about their clients they have at their fingertips, the better they can serve them. ACT!, GoldMine, and Microsoft Outlook are several programs that work nicely for this purpose. You must purchase a system (software), acclimate yourself to it, and then have the discipline to enter the information as you collect it. I know how hard this can be, because I'm a two-finger typist who doesn't enjoy busywork. But I can tell you that these tools are invaluable for success in sales relationships.

When you have a database of client profiles, you can anticipate their future needs. Auto salespeople will know how many years ago their clients bought and what they liked, so they can suggest new models at the appropriate time (after two to three years, for example). Financial services salespeople can highlight a businessperson's insurance and investment needs in advance at each point of their career. Medical devices salespeople can track surgeons who relocate to different hospitals and use that relationship to sell to a new buyer. This kind of attentive follow-up leads to clients who stay with you for the long haul.

Mr. Fix-It

Another method for deepening relationships with buyers is to turn client complaints into client kudos. Sales superstars become Mr. Fix-It whenever their clients have problems with their products. They repair any complaint with such determination and speed that their clients move from irritation to amazement.

> *Words that do not match deeds are not important.*
> **—CHE GUEVARA**

Mr. Fix-It knows that clients are always right—even when they aren't—because only the client's perception matters. Top pros use good listening skills (Chapter 3) and allow clients to convey their concerns and problems without interruption. Mr. Fix-It knows that clients need empathy, not sympathy, and that they absolutely hate to hear, "That's company policy." Mr. Fix-It uses the principle of relational banking and apologizes courteously. He doesn't rely on customer service or any other support personnel to apologize or accept responsibility (even if it's their fault). Mr. Fix-It knows, as Harry Truman used to say, that the buck stops with the sales professional. Sales superstars own the problem, apologize without hesitation, and resolve it immediately.

Kevin M., a sales rep with the ASP division of Johnson & Johnson, showed how to behave like Mr. Fix-It. An ASP sterilizer had broken down at a client hospital in California, which threatened to cancel the following week's surgical procedures. The potential lost revenue and the number of patient lives affected made this a serious situation, but Kevin had such a strong fix-it mindset that he immediately owned the problem, apologized to the surgical director, and told her he would contact her within three hours. For the next two and a half hours, Kevin fought hard to persuade his regional manager, the national manager, and ultimately the president that this was a golden opportunity to turn a serious client catastrophe into client kudos.

A 700-pound replacement sterilizer arrived at the hospital the following morning (a Saturday), along with the clinical and technical people to install and validate it. By Monday, it was ready to process surgical instruments, and the surgery schedule came off without a hitch. The surgical director, surgeons, and hospital administrators were overwhelmed by how Kevin and ASP had spared no expense or effort to resolve the problem. The director was so wowed that she wrote Kevin a beautiful letter and even invited him to dinner. Mr. Fix-It surpassed his client's expectations of service and created a loyal customer.

Leave 'Em with a Little Lagniappe

Another type of superior service that builds loyal relationships with your clients is to leave 'em with a little lagniappe. It's the customer service philosophy of providing your clients with a little something extra or an unexpected gift. *Lagniappe* is a Louisiana French Cajun word that means "an unexpected extra." It's the baker's dozen, the feel-good freebie, the bonus coupon, the surprise homemade warm and gooey cookies on your hotel nightstand. The practice began in New Orleans when shopkeepers first bought and sold grain in a woolen bag called *la nappe.* To compensate for grain that got caught in the bottom or spilled out the top, merchants would provide the customer a little extra without charging them. They'd say, "C'est pour la nappe." ("This is for what was lost in the sack.")

Lagniappe deepens relationships and creates a good feeling that clients don't easily forget. The extra something should be memorable and thoughtful but not necessarily expensive. Business growth specialist Jeff Blackman likes to mention the time when his family had purchased a Ford Windstar minivan and then two weeks later received two deluxe, fold-out chairs in a handy tote bag. Nothing earth shattering—but completely unexpected. Jeff and his family loved the freebies. "Whoa. Cool stuff!" his kids exclaimed—they were ready to remain Ford customers.

My own experiences with lagniappe are chronicled in my first book, *Wise Moves.* I was returning from a speaking engagement when my new Audi suddenly conked out—totally. The dealer quickly sent a flatbed tow truck, apologized profusely, and provided a free loaner on the spot. That was great service—but the unexpected extra came from the service manager, who bought me lunch at the restaurant of my choice. My kung pao chicken tasted outstanding, partly because I was in such a good mood—Audi had left me with a little lagniappe.

Three weeks before this book's deadline, I ended up with two flat tires on my Audi after driving through a construction zone to get home. I called Audi, and again they sent another tow truck for me right away. They called the next day to say my car was ready, but with a busy training and writing schedule, I couldn't afford the two hours needed for the round trip. I was literally working double time, so I called and asked if someone could deliver the car at my expense. The mechanic said that because it was a Friday afternoon, it was unlikely, but he'd know for sure at noon. When I called again, he still had nobody available, but he told me to hang on the line. Two minutes later, the service manager himself got on the phone and said he would drive the car to my house personally so I could keep working. More lagniappe!

When he arrived, I thanked him and gave him a copy of *Wise Moves,* with instructions to read Chapter 39 (the story of Audi's previous lagniappe). I winked and said, "Audi has done it again!" The manager's lagniappe wowed me again, and he got some reverse lagniappe when I gave him the book. Will I ever speak highly of Audi again? I just did!

Collaborative Partnering

The pinnacle of buyer-seller relationships is creating clients who are so loyal that they not only refuse to take their business elsewhere but welcome the salesperson as a collaborative partner. This loyalty is the result of high-level trust that has matured over time through outstanding service and follow-up.

The most effective method for developing unbreakable client loyalty is to benchmark the best practices that have consistently satisfied your ideal clients in the past, while continuing to look for new, creative ways to serve them. What have you done in that past that has worked well to initiate clients into your own special club? Consider what level and type of follow-up leaves them feeling like you're Johnny "On-the-Spot" and what you've done to be Mr. Fix-It for all the problems that typically arise. How have you left clients with a little lagniappe that they're still talking about? You must develop a list of these *best practices for client retention*—they become your benchmark, your platinum standard, for customer service and client retention.

> *Customer satisfaction is worthless, customer loyalty is priceless.*
> **—JEFFREY GITOMER**

When we worked with the Betco Corporation, we identified their best practices for retaining their clients by interviewing most of their sales team, management, and several of their clients. Here's a portion of their best practices retention checklist for both their end users and distributor clients.

- Ensure timely delivery of products or equipment.
- Conduct full and timely training of all end user operators.
- Conduct periodic retraining when appropriate.
- Develop relationships at all levels of the end user account.
- Identify new sales opportunities based upon their ongoing diagnosis.
- Sign end users up for the Betco newsletter with productivity enhancement suggestions.
- Train, motivate, and coach distributor sales personnel.
- Conduct quarterly account reviews with Gold Distributor management (their ideal distributors).
- Create a scorecard to continue and remind distributors of value-added activities.

One of the most important standards for Betco, and many other companies, is a quarterly business review meeting with clients. One of the greatest advantages you have over your competition is knowing your clients better than they do. Regular meetings help you determine how effectively you wow your client, whether there are any service gaps, and what their future needs are. It also gives you an opportunity to position new products, secure referrals, and continue developing high-level trust.

By knowing your ideal buyer profile and by examining your current client relationships, those clients with whom you want to partner more formally will emerge over time. Particularly in complex selling environments, high client loyalty will move your very best clients from a professional relationship to a collaborative partnership.

In collaborative partnering, the client no longer sees you as merely a vendor supplying a product on either a one-time or repeat basis. Partnering involves a trusting and respectful relationship in which you are part of their organization's routine. You're sought out to assist them in improving their strategic business, client, and product processes. You're called upon to assist them in addressing future changes and challenges. You are necessary to their business.

Consultative partnering requires a commitment to a win-win philosophy and to understanding the clients' business processes and high-level problems so that you can help co-manage their business. Sales superstars shine at conducting ongoing research (see Chapter 3) that helps their clients resolve their business problems. They become invaluable partners, putting all their resources to work for the client.

Partnering gives you a big advantage because it increases your client share. Client share is the percentage of total possible business that any particular client could give you. From the viewpoint of your time and effort, greater client share is preferred to greater market share, because a larger market share can only be obtained by spending a lot less time with a lot more people. A larger client share, on the other hand, involves spending more time with fewer people (your ideal collaborative partners). Focusing on client share increases both the value of these partnerships and the corresponding sales results without requiring a greater investment of your time. In short, it means spreading yourself thicker instead of thinner.

Collaborative relationships built on high-level trust provide the biggest windfall in sales. They take a great deal of time to build, so you should cultivate only a couple of these annuity accounts in the beginning. Continue to deepen those relationships, and they will yield a sales bonanza in future years. Here's how such a partnership worked for Mark P., a sales superstar and manufacturer's representative in computer networking technologies.

Mark forged a 20-year relationship with a Chicago-based distributor that eventually evolved into a collaborative partnership because of his great service, consistent follow-up, and cutting-edge expertise. When one of the nation's largest retailers began to deploy new networking topologies, this distributor sought out Mark to present the application solution and process and supply some of the critical components. Mark's partnership with the distributor gave the distributor the competitive advantage they needed to partner with the gigantic retailer on a $10 million project. Because of Mark's loyalty to the distributor and vice versa, they met an unusually demanding application need.

How much did Mark's collaborative partnering pay off? Mark received a commission check in excess of $60,000 for the first wave of deployment and recently obtained commitment for another $250,000 in business through the same retailer and distributor. Wow! Converting clients into collaborative partners makes the pinnacle of buyer-seller relationships a great place to be. Here are the Power Boosters that give you a deep foundation for your skyscraper of sales success.

POWER BOOSTERS

- Create your own special club and creatively find ways to make your clients feel special and recognized.

- Put a contact-management system in place to follow up and be Johnny "On-the-Spot" for your clients.

- Customize your contact system to be able to enter client information from the Eight-Point Buyer Checklist.

- Commit to becoming Mr. Fix-It, and when a client problem arises, own it, apologize for it, and immediately fix it.

- Find two or three ways you can leave your best clients with a little lagniappe.

- Recommend to your company that they benchmark the best practices for client retention and loyalty. If they don't listen, do it for yourself.

- Identify two or three ideal clients with whom you've started a relationship who may be candidates for collaborative partnering (if applicable).

- Develop a strategic initiative (as part of your business plan) for developing one or more of the above targets into a collaborative partner.

WIDEN YOUR RELATIONAL FOUNDATION

On October 17, 2003, the final 60-meter spire dropped into place on top of the Taipei 101 Tower in Taiwan, making it the world's tallest skyscraper at 1,674 feet and surpassing Chicago's Sears Tower. The Taipei Tower, whose architectural design is based on a bamboo shoot, is the world's first and only "supertall" to be built on a highly active earthquake zone. The Asians believe that "one climbs higher to see further." To display such an awe-inspiring view on top of a structure that looms almost one-third of a mile high, the Taipei 101 Tower required a massive,

24,221-square-meter foundation plate. Just as the Sears Tower needed an incredibly deep foundation to withstand Chicago's conditions, the Taipei 101 Tower needed an unusually wide foundation to cope with earthquakes and typhoons.

Sales superstars also enjoy a view from the top. To enjoy the view of sales success, they form a superwide foundation of relationships in their sales territory through networking, advance marketing, Headliner marketing, and referrals. In large accounts or complex selling arenas, they expand their foundation by covering all the bases in terms of buying influences, especially the powerful C-level players (CEOs, CIOs, CFOs, COOs, presidents, and VPs). The selling elite even build a foundation of nonclient relationships to support their climb. Company personnel, team members, fellow salespeople, friends, and family are all crucial for building a foundational base wide enough to withstand earthquakes in the selling field.

Reach Out and Touch Everybody

Sales superstars know that it's whom they know and who knows them that build a strong network of relationships. Most people intuitively feel that their close relationships, their "strong ties," are the key to their success. Actually, just the opposite is true—your "weak ties" are more important for sales and business success. Your close ties tend to be very similar to you and have a similar network of contacts. But your weak ties, which generally include people with diverse and dissimilar backgrounds, open sales doors that otherwise would be closed to you. Your Rolodex and the Rolodexes of those people who reside in yours can leverage your relationship network with awesome power. The more potential buyers you have positive relationships with, the more likely you are to do business with them. You want to become a great networker—a "connector" in the terminology of Malcolm Gladwell's *The Tipping Point*. Connectors are people who know an extraordinary number of people and are masters of the weak tie.

Prosperity in life is derived more from who you know, not what you know.
—MARK VICTOR HANSEN

In sales, your network ultimately creates your net worth, because all business is done through people. The key to expanding your network is the same key you learned to use to leverage your reputation in Chapter 1: personal marketing. Remember that this relationship-building strategy includes advance marketing, personal contact marketing, and Headliner marketing.

Sales letter or fax campaigns, e-zines, or direct mailings are great ways to get your name in front of more people and ultimately meet new people. Attending association meetings, trade shows, and industry events are all effective ways to expand your relationship foundation. Identify an advocate list of those 25 to 40 people most likely to provide you with referrals and systematically work to secure those referrals. Writing an article or making a presentation for your industry also helps you develop new relationships.

Remember from Chapter 1: the salesperson with the largest Rolodex wins!

Cover All the Bases

To develop a wide foundation of relationships within an account, you've got to know who the players are. Sales superstars first determine how the buying decision will be made by uncovering the evaluation process criteria (Eight-Point Buyer Checklist) and by identifying all relevant buying influences and decision makers. These determinations are then factored into the development of their best account strategy.

Sales pros also investigate *who* really has the influencing power, because they know that titles or positional authority is not necessarily an indicator of purchasing power. They unravel the political power in complex selling situations. Finally, the selling elite cover all their bases by developing relationships with each of the buying influences, especially those with power.

Buying influences can occupy one of four roles. Sales masters meet with:

1. The *economic buyer* (usually a C-level executive), who has the final authority to release the money for purchase.

2. The *user buyer,* who personally uses or supervises use of the product or service.
3. Any *technical buyers,* who judge the specifications of the product and can act as gatekeepers.
4. Any *coaches* (commonly called champions), who stand to gain a personal win if the product is purchased.

Sales pros always work especially hard to establish relationships with the coach and the C-level executive.

The coach. Coaches believe that purchasing your product will result in a personal win for them and a corporate win for their organization, so they provide guidance for the sale. The larger the sale, the more critical they are to winning the business. They give you insider status and are a necessary precursor to collaborative partnering. The coach must be identified and developed to win large, complex, and long buying cycle business.

To cultivate a coach, you must have credibility with that person, the coach must have credibility with the other buying influences, and the coach must want your prescription. You must sell coaches on the idea that if they better prepare you to sell, they will gain both personal and corporate wins through the purchase. The company wins, the coach wins, and you win. As my fellow sales colleague Jim H. always says, it's a win-win-win!

The C-level player. You must sell to the C-level of CEOs, CIOs, CFOs, COOs, presidents, and VPs if you want to bring home the big sales and fend off competitive threats more easily. As Kyle W.'s story with the hospital administrators demonstrated, it's not always easy to forge relationships with C-level executives. You must make contact with the executive, using whatever means are available—creativity (like Kyle), sponsorship by one of your loyal C-level clients, an introduction by your coach, or a very targeted sales letter/fax and follow-up campaign. Anthony Parinello's book, *Selling to VITO: The Very Important Top Officer,* is an excellent resource for the last approach. Going over a subordinate's head to reach the C-level decision maker usually backfires.

After reaching C-level executives, you must communicate with them on their wavelength to build a relationship. Remember from Chapter 4,

"The Power of Rapport," that you must connect with them in their language. Technical benefits may matter to the technical buyer, but these are *big picture* people. They look at enhancing productivity, reducing risk, increasing sales or market share, or improving processes and margins. They're looking for strategic, political, and financial benefits. They have tons of problems and pain, but to connect with them, you must identify, diagnose, and link your prescription to the broader benefits they seek.

Developing relationships with C-level players also requires that you exhibit an executive demeanor. Model how they communicate, make decisions, and even dress. Read executive-focused periodicals like *Forbes, Fortune, BusinessWeek,* and *The Wall Street Journal* and digest books on executive-level topics and thought processes. Relationships with C-level executives lead to sales success.

Team Up to Win

When American military forces go into combat, individual soldiers often perform heroic acts. Love of their country, however, is not always what motivates them; instead, they behave heroically out of loyalty to their fellow soldiers. Basic training has drilled into them that they must never let their teammates down, and they perform beyond themselves when they're devoted to a greater purpose—to their team.

Sales superstars also know that success is never a solo act. Behind every great achiever is a team. This book was a team effort. Whatever company you work for or whatever you sell, there are people who want to help you become successful. These fellow salespeople, in-house personnel, family, and friends who want you to make it big are your team. The selling elite know that belonging to a team not only helps you be more resilient (Chapter 6) but also ignites your spirit to win.

Teams foster the competitive drive. We usually push ourselves much harder for a team we're committed to than we would for just ourselves. Being devoted to a purpose that reaches beyond ourselves brings out our very best.

Teams also leverage your resources for greater success. They foster *synergy*—where their members' ideas and goals interact with each other to produce strategies and methods that single members could never create alone. Synergistic teams find superior ways to outsell the competition, overcome market conditions, fix client problems, wow ideal clients, or even find new prospects.

Team spirit requires that you recognize your coworkers and managers who helped you make it to the top. Many hard-working administrative, marketing, finance, operations, manufacturing, and management personnel don't get to share the limelight that the star salesperson does. Thank your team—serve them a little lagniappe.

Another team relationship that can build sales success is a professional coach. No matter how committed we are or how much willpower we have, a coach can challenge us to step up and achieve more. My coaches have helped me find useful strategies and have held me accountable to the commitments I made to myself. Some of the greatest achievers like Michael Jordan, Tiger Woods, and Anthony Robbins all have used coaching to help them close the gap between where they are and where they wanted to be.

Personal relationships with family and friends are the cornerstone for a solid life plan that balances life and work. It's very easy in a sales career to neglect those whom we love and who love us. I know; I've been there. But at the end of our lives, we won't remember that one extra sale; we'll remember those moments shared with our children, significant others, family, and friends. They weave the richest tapestry of our lives.

Here is *Power Selling's* last list of Power Boosters to help you establish a wide and rewarding relational foundation.

POWER BOOSTERS

- Leverage advance marketing, networking, and Headliner marketing to establish more client and industry relationships.

- Develop your advocacy list for referrals and work to secure them.

- Make sure you identify who all the buying influences are and which ones have real power (for those complex selling situations).

- In complex selling situations, always try to cultivate a coach.

- Commit to developing a more executive demeanor and start calling on C-level decision makers.

- Commit to being a TEAM player.

- Take extra time to thank all those team members who support you every day on your journey to sales stardom.

- Consider sales coaching to assist you in elevating your performance.

- Commit to spending time and having fun with your family and friends, no matter what.

LET'S RECAP

Sales superstars know that relationships are the foundation for towering sales success. They love people and they love to provide incredible value to those whom they have the privilege to serve. Sales masters commit, deepen, and widen their foundation of relationships so that high-level trust, client loyalty, collaborative partnering, and sales stardom can be realized.

Sales relationships are opened by closing the sale and obtaining commitment and then are deepened by exceeding client expectations on a consistent basis. Client loyalty and collaborative partnering are the final rewards for mature, time-tested relationships built on trust, competence, and outstanding service. The selling elite also never forget their teammates, friends, and family, because they know success is not a solo act.

Cracking the sales code has been accomplished in *Power Selling* by peering into the electron microscope to discover all seven strands of a sales superstar's DNA. *Reputation, real passion, research, rapport, resource management,* and *resiliency* are all in the genetic makeup. On the seventh and final strand of DNA, we find the Power of Relationships.

In or around October 1805, an old man stood near the edge of a sizable river in Northern Virginia. It was cold and he needed to get to the other side, but there were no bridges. After waiting most of the morning for someone who might be able to help him get across, he was delighted when he saw five riders emerge from the woods on horseback.

The old man let the first rider go by and said nothing. He let the second, third, and fourth riders pass without saying a word. Finally, when the fifth rider came abreast, the old man looked at him and said, "Mister, could I please ride with you to the other side?"

The rider, with no hesitation whatsoever, said, "Climb aboard, my friend." When they finally reached the other side of the cold river safely, the old man dismounted and regained his footing. Before the rider left, he asked the old man why he had let the other four riders pass by.

The old man responded, "When I looked into their eyes, I could see no kindness, I could see no caring, so I knew they would not help me. But when I looked into your eyes, I could see the kindness, I could see the caring, and I knew that you would help me across that cold river."

After hearing that, the rider said, "Thank you for your kind words. I'll remember them." And with that, my boyhood hero, Thomas Jefferson, turned his horse and rode off in the direction of the White House.

They say that the eyes are the windows to the soul. What do the people you are in a relationship with—clients, teammates, friends, and family—see and feel when they look in *your* eyes?

PUTTING THE POWERS TO WORK

The Power Selling Process

Give us the tools and we will finish the job.
—WINSTON CHURCHILL

Legend has it that an old man, on the last day of a long musical career, sat hunched over an organ, all alone in a cathedral while he played his last bit of music. A young man quietly appeared without much fanfare at the back of the cathedral and made his way toward the organ. When he reached the old man, he said nothing but slowly extended his hand with an open palm. The old man ceased playing, reluctantly pulled out the organ's giant key, and gently set it in the young man's hand. The old man shuffled slowly toward the door, sad about ending his career and turning over the key to his replacement. As he was about to leave, he heard the young man begin to play. The old man turned around in amazement and stood spellbound while he listened to the beautiful music, tears rolling down his cheeks. He had turned his key over to a man by the name of Wolfgang Amadeus Mozart.

In this final chapter, you'll receive the key to producing great "sales music" with the strategies of *Power Selling*. With this key that I present you, you'll be able to take the precious time that you've invested in learning the strategies of the world's greatest salespeople and become one yourself. My hope is that you *don't* get your money's worth from this book—my hope is that you get *more* than your money's worth! I want this book both to remind you of what you've forgotten and teach you new skills, too. Your sales career and your life will be enriched forever if you meet the challenges they present.

This final chapter has two objectives: first, to share a systematic process *(the key)* so that you can take all seven strategies for sales success and apply them in an easy and effective way; second, to provide a call to arms to boldly march forth and claim your "Sales Oscar" and your place in the sales superstars' hall of fame.

> *Systems theory looks at the world in terms of the interrelatedness of all phenomena, and in this framework an integrated whole whose properties cannot be reduced to those parts is called a system.*
> **—FRITJOF CAPRA**

While most people are familiar with the terms *Industrial Revolution, Technological Revolution,* and *Information Revolution,* the term *Turn-Key Revolution* usually elicits a blank stare. However, the Turn-Key Revolution, as described by Michael Gerber in his book, *The E-Myth Revisited,* has had a staggering effect on American business. Gerber attributes the influx of massive entrepreneurial success to the franchising process first orchestrated on a grand scale by Ray Kroc. In less than 40 years, Ray Kroc's McDonald's restaurants have become more than a $25 billion a year business with over 15,000 restaurants around the world. His model of franchising—implementing a repeatable business system—represents more than 42 percent of every retail dollar spent in America.

McDonald's franchisees don't buy only the name; they buy a proven process to do business—a turn-key for success. They follow an organized system that produces predictable results, no matter what their location. That business system is created by combining the best practices from every aspect of the business into a sequenced process that consistently yields positive results. This explains why less than 5 percent of franchisees operating with a proven system are terminated within their first five years, while more than 80 percent of independently owned business start-ups fail.

Success in sales today depends as much on the system used to sell a product as the product itself. Salespeople need a franchise system that creates a foolproof methodology for predictable sales results. That system is the Power Selling Process. We've taught thousands of salespeople to use this process—it's the best process for sales success available.

Many corporations hire me to teach this sales system to their sales team because they realize the importance of having a sustainable sales platform framed around a set of best practices that follows a systematic strategic approach. They want what Dan Carr, vice president of sales for the Betco Corporation, described when he said, "We need a sales process that is easy, logical, visible, and most importantly, repeatable." The Power Selling Process is that process, and it can be customized to work for pharmaceutical, health care, real estate, insurance, financial services, and countless other industries.

In reading the seven chapters of this book, you've had to digest a *large* amount of information. The key to putting all that knowledge to work is having a structure or framework that organizes it in a way that makes it easy to use. The Power Selling Process provides you with a system—a franchise—that sequences the skill sets you've learned in the seven strategies. It enables you to conceptualize your sales efforts as a process with five stages, each with specific tasks and goals. Locating yourself in that process from the beginning to the end of a sale organizes what you need to do and when you need to do it and gives you ready access to your newly acquired sales knowledge and tactics.

The Power Selling Process is unique among the many sales process models offered by trainers and consultants today. It is the only system we've seen that includes a stage devoted to retaining clients through building unbreakable client loyalty. It also guides you in deciding where to put your greatest energy and efforts in the course of a sale. As you can see from the diagram in Figure C.1, obtaining commitment (or closing the sale) should receive the least amount of your attention. Students of older, more traditional sales models may be shocked to learn that having the buyer actually make the purchase is the *least* important step of the selling process, but it's true—if you've done your work properly up to that point, you'll need to devote very little energy to getting the order.

The Power Selling Process teaches you to work the hardest *before* you ever even meet the buyer—the identification stage of the diagram is the launching pad for the whole process. Gathering critical information that allows you to identify the ideal prospects and strategies is the step that leads to the greatest success.

Finally, the Power Selling Process will help you always keep your focus *on* the client and *off* your product. Anybody can get enthusiastic about an exciting product, but it takes a pro to understand that what really motivates someone to buy is knowing how that product will solve a problem or provide growth. Our model keeps your focus on the client and your sales numbers soaring.

The Power Selling Process has five sequential phases. In any given sale, especially in complex selling environments, you may find yourself working on two different phases at the same time or needing to return

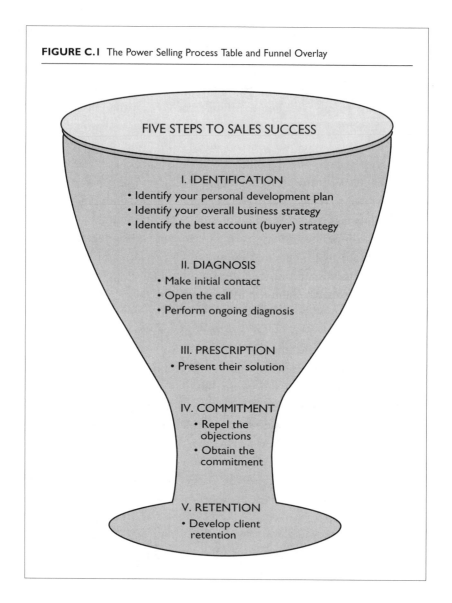

FIGURE C.I The Power Selling Process Table and Funnel Overlay

FIVE STEPS TO SALES SUCCESS

I. IDENTIFICATION
• Identify your personal development plan
• Identify your overall business strategy
• Identify the best account (buyer) strategy

II. DIAGNOSIS
• Make initial contact
• Open the call
• Perform ongoing diagnosis

III. PRESCRIPTION
• Present their solution

IV. COMMITMENT
• Repel the objections
• Obtain the commitment

V. RETENTION
• Develop client retention

to a previous stage temporarily. The process, however, will continue to orient you and organize your sales efforts. All of the strategic and tactical moves necessary to complete each stage have already been presented in this book and draw from one or more of the seven powers. After a brief description of each phase, the tactical moves required to meet its goals will be listed in bullet format.

THE POWER SELLING PROCESS

Identification

This first phase of the sales process should command your greatest energy and attention. You must identify in advance everything necessary that will increase your chances of being successful, such as your personal development plan, your overall business strategy, and the best account strategy for each buyer. This homework is generally done before ever engaging the buyer, but it's the most crucial step, because the entire rest of the process collapses without it. No matter how great your product is, if you're putting it in front of the wrong people with the wrong strategy, you won't make the sale.

Sales identification takes place at three levels: the personal level, the territory or business level, and the buyer or account level. Identification includes all of the following.

Identify your personal development plan.

- Life plan (purpose statement, personal goals, and time management)
- C-CORE development (competence, confidence, commitment, and character)
- Limiting beliefs, habitually pessimistic responses, fears, or slumps to overcome
- Sales skills development (commitment to PANG)
- Strategies for becoming *the* industry specialist
- Rituals for supercharging your selling state (psychology and physiology)
- Daily prime-time rituals (for all of the above)

Identify your overall business strategy.

- Ideal buyer profile checklist
- *Targeted conversations* for ideal buyers by title
- Ideal buyer account target list
- Market position assessment
- Sales volume goals
- Ideal sales day
- Sales funnel analysis and prioritization (law of the farm)
- Strategic time management and daily critical few
- Prospecting plan (advance marketing, in-person marketing, Headliner marketing, cold calling, etc.)
- Telephone and face-to-face engagement scripts
- Advocate list for referral and testimonial generation
- Networking and relationship-building tactics
- Reputation-enhancing tactics
- Client-retention tactics
- Contact-management tactics
- Administrative duties

Identify the best account strategy.

- Research the buyer's organization
- All buying influences (including C-level buyers)
- Coach or potential coach to be developed
- Predicted buyer response mode
- Account sales objectives
- Account precall tactics (including your selling state)
- Engagement tactics (prospecting, including referrals)

Average sales reps don't plan to fail; they fail because they failed to plan. This phase lays the groundwork for the rest of every sale and gives you a winning plan.

Diagnosis

The second phase of the sales process, in which you engage the buyer with the intent of diagnosing their pain or desire for gain, is where you begin to demonstrate your commitment to focusing on the client instead of your product. You begin by establishing rapport and uncovering all of their critical wants and needs. You establish credibility in this phase primarily by asking questions and listening to the answers.

Diagnosis of both the buyer and their organization must include face-to-face meetings with all buying influences, especially if it's a complex selling situation. The Power Selling Process, unlike most other models, emphasizes that you *never* prescribe a product, service, or solution until you've completed a thorough diagnosis (even if the buyer is impatient to proceed) and the buyer has confirmed your diagnosis. You must earn the right to proceed. Sales diagnosis can generally be broken down into three steps: making initial contact, opening the call, and the ongoing diagnosis. Diagnosis includes the following steps.

Make initial contact.

- Contact the buyer by phone for an appointment.
- Be in the supercharged selling state.
- Follow the telephone engagement rules.
- Stick to your telephone engagement script.
- Establish rapport.
- Securing the appointment is the goal.
- Use your 15-second to 30-second infomercial as needed.
- Use RPM Questioning as needed.

Open the call.

- Engage the buyer face-to-face.
- Follow the face-to-face rules of engagement.
- Be in the supercharged selling state.
- Establish rapport using as many rapport builders as possible.
- Use your infomercial or reference success stories as needed.

Perform ongoing diagnosis.

- Take the oath to become a Doctor of Selling.
- Meet all the buying influences face-to-face.
- Unravel the political power in complex sales situations.

- Follow the RPM Questioning model.
  - ✓ *Reality.* Confirm your identification and assess the situation.
  - ✓ *Pain-gain.* Uncover the pain or desire for gain.
  - ✓ *Magnification.* Intensify the pain or desire for gain.
- Use great listening skills (golden silence).
- Follow the Eight-Point Buyer Checklist.
- Determine the buyer's need level (individual and account).
- Discover both personal and corporate wins.
- Confirm the diagnosis before moving to the prescription phase.

The diagnosis phase keeps your focus where it should be—on the client and off your product. Only when buyers know that you're mostly concerned with *their* needs will they begin to consider your solution.

Prescription

In this third phase of the sales process, you use your accurate diagnosis to share the benefits that your product or service provides. Cutting corners in the diagnosis phase leads to an inappropriate prescription, wasting both your and the buyer's time. During prescription, you continue to use questions to magnify the buyer's pain and use your presentation skills, including reference stories, to magnify your product or service as *the* solution. You must also offer the necessary proof so that the buyer *sees and confirms your solution.*

Using your *supercharged selling state* in this phase transfers your enthusiasm and energy for your product directly to the buyer. You must become *a state prompter* so that buyers link *their buying state* to your solution. Even though this is the step where you actually present your product, you must continue to focus on the client—never seek commitment for the order without confirming that the buyer agrees with the prescription. The prescription phase centers on presenting your solution and includes the following steps.

Present their solution.

- Be in the supercharged selling state.
- Present from a foundation of research and rapport.

- Be able to differentiate between features, advantages, and benefits.
- Work from a developed list of probable benefits (differentiated, too).
- Present only those benefits the buyer has stated are important.
- Demonstrate capability with product demo or evaluation.
- Use M questions to magnify the pain of not purchasing the solution.
- Use M questions to magnify the benefits of the solution.
- Use reference success stories so the buyer sees the solution.
- Use the success stories, references who can be called, your client list, and testimonial letters as proof sources.
- Offer value justification as necessary.
- Present to as many of the buyer's senses as possible.
- Get potential buyers physically involved.
- Confirm the prescription before attempting to obtain commitment.

The prescription phase creates a vision of your solution in the minds of potential buyers that prompts them not only to see and agree with that solution but to actually initiate purchase themselves.

Commitment

Unlike many other sales systems, the Power Selling Process deemphasizes the point at which closing occurs. If you've followed our model closely in the first three phases, you'll need to devote very little effort to obtain a commitment to purchase or advance the process in a complex sale—buyers themselves will be ready to take that step. You've already identified a buyer whom you could serve, diagnosed the area of pain accurately, and confirmed that diagnosis with the buyer. You have prescribed a solution and confirmed with the buyer that this prescription was *the* solution. You're then ready for the next logical step—the order. Obtaining this commitment from the potential buyer moves the buyer-seller relationship to the next level.

The commitment phase is also where you must handle objections, but the Power Selling Process greatly reduces the chances that you'll hear any in the first place. Trouble in this phase arises when a salesperson attempts to close an order prematurely, which leads to a breakdown in trust and credibility. Commitment can be separated into two primary areas: repelling objections and obtaining commitment.

Repel the objections.

- Prevent objections by following the Power Selling Process.
- Don't present benefits that are not important to the buyer.
- Handle early objections by diagnosing more effectively.
- Handle late objections (value objections) with benefit statements.
- Handle late objections with reference success stories.
- Empathize with potential buyers and reassure their purchase decision.

Obtain the commitment.

- Be politely persistent.
- Don't seek commitment unless it's committable.
- Be a keen observer for verbal and nonverbal buying signals.
- Avoid answering questions with a yes or no.
- Follow the three steps for obtaining commitment.
  1. Confirm that their concerns have been met.
  2. Restate your prescription's benefits.
  3. Propose or ask for the commitment.
- Once you've asked for commitment: shut up!
- After they purchase, celebrate the sale and the opening of a new client relationship.
- Commit to the client relationship.

The Power Selling Process teaches you to think, not about closing a sale, but about opening a long-term relationship with the buyer. This is just a logical extension of the steps you've followed and doesn't require extensive effort on your part. Many sales systems teach lots of closing techniques and maneuvers; the Power Selling Process simply keeps your focus on the client, where it's been all along.

Retention

The Power Selling Process includes a fifth and vital phase that most sales models neglect. Retention takes your ideal buyers and turns them into long-term, loyal clients who return to you for continued business. This phase requires a significant investment of your time and energy and is based on great service to your clients over a long period of time. Again, our process directs you toward your buyers and their needs.

Client loyalty is a *state*. An account cannot be loyal—only the people who manage the account can be. Loyalty develops when outstanding customer service, based on identified best practices, builds trust over time. When relationships with loyal clients are nurtured through continued service and follow-up, ideal clients can join you at the summit of buyer-seller relationships—collaborative partnering. Collaborative relationships built on high-level trust provide the maximum leverage of time and effort and bring the biggest results, because it's always more difficult to sell a new buyer than it is to retain a current client. Loyal clients also provide you with immunity from competition. Achieving client retention involves the following techniques.

Develop client retention.

- Adopt a client-centric focus on serving.
- Identify best practices for client loyalty and retention.
- Develop a best practices checklist for client retention.
- Execute best client retention practices consistently.
- Use your contact-management system for follow-up.
- Be "Johnny On-the-Spot."
- Be Mr. Fix-It to handle all client problems and complaints as soon as possible.
- Create your own special club.
- Find ways to leave clients with a little lagniappe.
- Identify potential accounts for collaborative partnering.
- Conduct regular account reviews with targeted accounts.

The Power Selling Process places a high priority on client retention. The effort you expend in this phase will yield the biggest windfalls as you rack up the repeat business.

This process gives you the key to applying the seven *Power Selling* strategies in a systematic manner to become a sales superstar. It guides your decisions about *what* you should do and *when* you should do it. The steps that other sales models stress as being most important will not produce the best sales results; instead, you must keep your focus on the buyer and invest your energy in the steps that will lead to continued sales.

AND THE WINNER IS . . .

Imagine for a minute walking down a red carpet with your family, friends, and company cheering you on. You exceeded your sales goals and are enjoying the money and recognition you deserve. Whether you're a corporate salesperson, entrepreneur, or CEO, your name is in lights, and tonight you'll collect a sales trophy, just like an Oscar, with your name on it. Bravo! Bravo! You made it, you *cracked the sales code*, you unleashed the seven strategies of the sales superstars, and you have become a celebrity in your world.

Your imagination is the preview to life's coming attractions.
—ALBERT EINSTEIN

Now that was just fantasy—but it doesn't have to be! We've come a long way, together. How much further you go will be your decision. This book has given you the tools, skills, and ideas that can make you a distinguished member of the selling elite. If you apply what you've read, you'll be collecting your sales trophy from the awards ceremony called life. You can put this book down—as we've all done before—knowing that you learned something and then go on as you have been. Or you can decide now to create a more favorable future. It will only happen if you make it happen. Your destiny is your choice.

You now know the sales code—the seven strategies for selling excellence. You know that the power of *reputation, real passion, research, rapport, resource management, resiliency,* and *relationships* can dramatically change your income, your happiness, and your life. You now have the Power Selling Process to assist you in deploying the seven strategies in an easy, logical, and repeatable system. You also have the online assessment questionnaire to track your progress as well as the other online resources available at http://www.powersellingbook.com. Like young Mozart, you now have the keys to sales success.

In life, we don't get what we want; we get who we become.
—GEORGE LUDWIG

Many salespeople will never become superstars because they won't change. They hope that "the world out there" will change for the better. It rarely does. The lesson is simple: you can become a member of the selling elite only by understanding the strategies of the selling game and then taking action to apply them. The seven powers of *Power Selling* and the Power Selling Process are the strategies of the game, but you must apply them. Carlos Castaneda summed it up this way.

> You should know by now that a man of knowledge lives by acting, not by thinking about acting, nor by thinking about what he will think when he has finished acting. A man of knowledge chooses a path with heart and follows it.

This book will work for you if you apply it with gusto. You can't become a sales master half-heartedly or by being partially engaged. You can't stroll to your goal.

Sales superstars never let their dreams die. Despite a slump, a bad economy, getting fired, or whatever bad cards they've been dealt (or have dealt themselves), they always believe they can reach their dreams. They know that if others can reach their dreams, they can, too.

But following your dream requires persistence. Calvin Coolidge said it so beautifully.

> Press on. Nothing can take the place of persistence. Talent will not; the world is full of unsuccessful people with talent. Genius will not; unrewarded genius is almost a proverb. Education will not; the world is full of educated derelicts. Persistence and determination alone are omnipotent.

Following your dream also requires being bold—bold enough to do whatever it takes to make it. To live your dream, reach your goal, improve your life, or become a sales superstar, you must leave the *comfort zone* for the *bold zone*, where you spark a fire within, where there's a will to win and an unstoppable spirit.

Living in the comfort zone is like sitting by the edge of the pool when you're afraid to get in. You want to know how deep the water is, how cold it is, and who's on duty as lifeguard. Fagetaboutit—dive in! Getting out of the comfort zone and breaking through to the bold zone is not easy. It can't be done overnight. But it always starts with just a single, determined step. You must summon your courage, make the leap, take the plunge, and leave hesitation behind. Sales stardom awaits those who boldly apply *Power Selling's* strategies.

My first sales mentor, Bill, did more than inspire me to crack the DNA code of sales superstars. He also taught me to be bold. Bill was at my side one day in a Chicago hospital as I pushed a big cart of defibrillators and monitoring equipment through the hallway. We passed a large set of doors near the surgery department that was covered by very intimidating red and white stripes and had an unfriendly sign that read: DO NOT ENTER. AUTHORIZED PERSONNEL ONLY.

As I started to push the cart past the doors, Bill gestured toward them and told me to take the cart through them. I responded, "Bill, we can't go in there. It says, 'Do not enter.' We might get thrown out."

Bill then asked me a question I would never forget. "How much business will you get from behind those doors if you don't push in there?"

"Zero," I said.

Bill replied, "Exactly. And what's the worst that could happen if we *do* push in there and get thrown out?"

"We won't get their business, I guess," I said.

"And would we be any worse off than if we'd never gone in?"

"Well, no—because we wouldn't have their business anyway," I replied.

Then Bill said something else that sank in. "When you try something new, the worst that can happen is that you end up where you started—you haven't lost anything. But if you're bold and try a new approach, a lot of times you'll get rewarded."

Nervously, I pushed the cart through the doors, and sure enough, a large, unfriendly looking, authoritative nurse approached rapidly. She descended upon us and snarled, "What do you need, boys?" Before I could say anything, I got another lesson from Bill.

Bill flashed a big grin and said, "Well, actually, we need some coffee. He takes cream and sugar, I like mine black, and we have some new monitoring equipment we're *supposed* to show you."

A bit bowled over and reeling from Bill's bold approach, I was shocked and elated when she began laughing and said, "You've sure got some spunk. Come on in here, let me get the coffee, and sure, I'll give you *just* five minutes to show me what you've got."

Thirty-five minutes later, we walked away with a great lead for two defibrillators and the start of a new client relationship. Bill showed me that day that you really have nothing to lose by being bold and everything to lose if you don't take the chance. The ultimate message of this book is to take the plunge and apply the seven strategies to your sales career. That's the only way they'll get fully anchored in your DNA's makeup. Improving your sales ability always starts with a bold initiative.

My wish is for you to experience great success, prosperity, happiness, and fulfillment. I hope we get to meet someday, but until then—may the power of selling be with you!

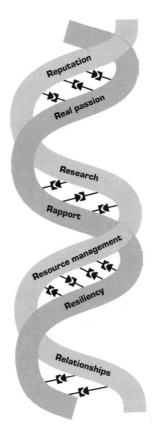

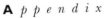

SAMPLE PURPOSE STATEMENT

(*Mission, Vision, and Credo*)

GEORGE LUDWIG'S
2004 PURPOSE STATEMENT

I love God, my family, my friends, myself, and everyone I have the privilege to affect. I contribute my talents, time, and finances to helping those who are under-resourced.

I am superhealthy and fit, bringing high energy to all that I do. I am cheerful and optimistic, showing gratitude for life. I am gaining intelligence and wisdom by constantly learning and growing. I am using that knowledge to serve others better and enjoy the journey more. I live with passion by pursuing my goals and feeding my mind positive mental thoughts every day. I fuel that passion by maintaining a powerful physiology every day.

I serve others through my gifts of speaking, consulting, selling, writing, and making people laugh. I am an agent of change determined to help as many people as possible break through to a life of greater achievement, fulfillment, prosperity, and happiness.

I am achieving great financial wealth so I can have more choices on the planet, inspire others more effectively, and contribute more to those in need. And finally, I am living as a child, always looking for fun, adventure, toys, and lots of laughter!

SAMPLE IDEAL BUYER PROFILE CHECKLIST

(Betco Corporation)

1. The buyer is in a targeted market segment (education, health care, retail, manufacturing, or building services contractors).
2. There is more than $10,000 potential annual sales volume.
3. There is a receptive buyer response mode (visible need or compelling dormant need).
4. There is an acceptable margin potential.
5. An existing competitive contract doesn't preclude business opportunity.
6. The potential buyer needs are in alignment with Betco's strengths (floor care, equipment, and chemical management).
7. There is a solid distributor relationship in place.
8. The potential buyer is not predominantly a "price shopper."
9. There is access to all buying influences (economic, technical, user, and coach).

Personal Development

Allen, James. *As a Man Thinketh.* CA: DeVorss and Co., 1983.

Bridges, William. *The Way of Transition: Embracing Life's Most Difficult Moments.* Cambridge: Perseus Publishing, 2001.

Chopra, Deepak. *Ageless Body, Timeless Mind: The Quantum Alternative to Growing Old.* New York: Harmony Books, 1993.

Covey, Stephen R. *The Seven Habits of Highly Effective People.* New York: Simon & Schuster, 1990.

Csikszentmihalyi, Mihaly. *Flow: The Psychology of Optimal Experience.* New York: HarperCollins, 1990.

Diamond, Marilyn, and Donald Burton Schnell. *Fitonics for Life.* New York: Avon Books, 1996.

Dyer, Wayne W. *Wisdom of the Ages: 60 Days to Enlightenment.* New York: HarperCollins, 1998.

———. *Your Erroneous Zones.* New York: HarperCollins, 1976.

Frankl, Viktor E. *Man's Search for Meaning.* New York: Simon & Schuster, 1946.

Goleman, Daniel. *Emotional Intelligence: Why It Can Matter More Than IQ.* New York: Bantam Books, 1995.

Ludwig, George. *Wise Moves: 60 Quick Tips to Improve Your Position in Life & Business.* Chicago: CRL Publishing, 2003.

McGraw, Phillip C. *Self Matters: Creating Your Life from the Inside Out.* New York: Simon & Schuster, 2001.

Peck, M. Scott. *The Road Less Traveled.* New York: Simon & Schuster, 1978.

Robbins, Anthony. *Awaken the Giant Within: How to Take Immediate Control of Your Mental, Emotional, Physical, and Financial Destiny.* New York: Simon & Schuster, 1991.

———. *Unlimited Power: The New Science of Personal Achievement.* New York: Ballantine Books, 1986.

Seligman, Martin E.P. *Authentic Happiness: Using the New Positive Psychology to Realize Your Potential for Lasting Fulfillment.* New York: Simon & Schuster, 2002.

———. *Learned Optimism: How to Change Your Mind and Your Life.* New York: Simon & Schuster, 1990.

Weil, Andrew. *Eight Weeks to Optimum Health.* New York: Alfred A. Knopf, 1997.

The Holy Bible.

Business, Marketing, and Leadership

Beckwith, Harry. *Selling the Invisible: A Field Guide to Modern Marketing.* New York: Warner Books, 1997.

Collins, James C. *Good to Great: Why Some Companies Make the Leap . . . and Others Don't.* New York: HarperCollins, 2001.

Gerber, Michael E. *The E-Myth Revisited: Why Most Small Businesses Don't Work and What to Do about It.* New York: HarperCollins, 1995.

Gladwell, Malcolm. *The Tipping Point: How Little Things Can Make a Big Difference.* New York: Little, Brown and Company, 2000.

Godin, Seth. *Purple Cow: Transform Your Business by Being Remarkable.* New York: Penguin Group, 2002.

Maxwell, John C. *The 21 Immutable Laws of Leadership*. Nashville: Thomas Nelson, 1998.

Moore, Geoffrey A. *Crossing the Chasm*. New York: Harper Business 1995.

———. *Inside the Tornado: Marketing Strategies from Silicon Valley's Cutting Edge*. New York: Harper Business 1995.

Peters, Tomas J., and Robert H. Waterman, Jr. *In Search of Excellence*. New York: Warner Books, 1988.

Ries, Al, and Jack Trout. *The 22 Irrefutable Laws of Marketing*. New York: HarperCollins, 1993.

Singletary, Mike, and Rick DeMarco. *The Leadership Zone*. Naperville, IL: Inside Advantage Publications, 2003.

Selling

Bosworth, Michael T. *Solution Selling: Creating Buyers in Difficult Selling Markets*. New York: McGraw-Hill, 1995.

Carnegie, Dale. *How to Win Friends and Influence People*. New York: Simon & Schuster, 1991.

Duncan, Todd M. *High Trust Selling: Make More Money—In Less Time—with Less Stress*. Nashville: Thomas Nelson, 2002.

Frank, Milo O. *How to Get Your Point Across in 30 Seconds or Less*. New York: Simon & Schuster, 1986.

Gitomer, Jeffrey H. *The Sales Bible: The Ultimate Sales Resource*. New York: William Morrow, 1994.

Hopkins, Tom. *How to Master the Art of Selling*. New York: Warner Books, 1980.

Mandino, Og. *The Greatest Salesman in the World*. New York: Bantam Books, 1968.

Miller, Robert B., and Stephen E. Heiman. *Strategic Selling*. New York: Warner Books, 1986.

Page, Rick. *Hope Is Not a Strategy: The 6 Keys to Winning the Complex Sale*. Atlanta: Nautilus Press, 2002.

Parinello, Anthony. *Selling to VITO (the Very Important Top Offer)*. Holbrook, MA: Adams Media, 1994.

Rackham, Neil. *SPIN Selling*. New York: McGraw-Hill, 1988.

Schiffman, Stephan. *Cold Calling Techniques (That Really Work!)*. Holbrook, MA: Adams Media, 1987.

Tracy, Brian, *Advanced Selling Strategies: The Proven System of Sales Ideas, Methods, and Techniques Used by Top Salespeople*. New York: Simon & Schuster, 1995.

Willingham, Ron. *Integrity Selling: How to Succeed in the Competitive Years Ahead*. New York: Doubleday, 1987.

Ziglar, Zig. *Ziglar on Selling: The Ultimate Handbook for the Complete Sales Professional*. New York: Ballantine Books, 1991.

A

B

George Ludwig is a national authority on peak performance and sales success, and is a highly sought-after consultant. He's the author of *Wise Moves: 60 Quick Tips to Improve Your Position in Life & Business*. Ludwig has more than 25 years of sales, sales management, sales training, and seminar presentation experience across the country.

Ludwig's client list includes Johnson & Johnson, Sprint, Bank One, Mazda North America, Southwest Airlines, Northwestern Mutual, Coldwell Banker, and Century 21. He's frequently interviewed for trade publications and newspapers, including *Selling Power* magazine, *Sales & Marketing Management, Entrepreneur, Investors Business Daily, Time,* and *The New York Times,* as well as for talk radio shows.

Mr. Ludwig lives along the scenic Fox River, near Chicago, Illinois.

GLU CONSULTING

GLU Consulting, founded in 2001, works with business leaders who want to improve their company's performance, and with individuals who want to grow personally and professionally. The GLU approach revolves around a simple premise: improving the client's condition.

Resources for Organizational Improvement

Our key to success is our creative ability to redirect existing talents and resources to increase sales, enhance customer loyalty, and achieve business goals. Our collaborative work involves client personnel and the transfer of skills to the client. We work toward specific objectives with clearly established outcomes and timing, contributing to client business goals. We offer:

- Sales, customer service, and marketing expertise
- "Best practices" identification and benchmarking
- Process development and performance improvement
- Sales process and sales skills training
- Performance improvement training
- Keynote speaking

Resources for Personal Growth and Sales Success

- Books and e-books
- Audio programs
- Fast-track tele-seminars
- Coaching services

For more information regarding any of the services or products being offered by George Ludwig Unlimited, visit http://www.georgeludwig.com, or call 888-999-4811.